Song

of the

Sea

One woman's journey through love
and loss to find her voice with
The Fishwives Choir

JANE DOLBY

This edition first published in Great Britain in 2015 by
Orion
an imprint of the Orion Publishing Group Ltd
Orion House, 5 Upper St Martin's Lane,
London WC2H 9EA
An Hachette UK Company

1 3 5 7 9 10 8 6 4 2

A CIP catalogue record for this book is available
from the British Library.

Mass Market Paperback ISBN: 978 1 4091 5347 4

Typeset at The Spartan Press Ltd,
Lymington, Hants

Printed and bound by the CPI Group (UK) Ltd,
Croydon, CR0 4YY

The Orion Publishing Group's policy is to use papers
that are natural, renewable and recyclable and made from wood
grown in sustainable forests. The logging and manufacturing
processes are expected to conform to the environmental
regulations of the country of origin.

Every effort has been made to fulfil requirements with regard to
reproducing copyright material. The author and publisher will be
glad to rectify any omissions at the earliest opportunity.

www.orionbooks.co.uk

For my four children with all my love.
May your anchors hold in the storms of life.

Prologue

'**D**ance to your daddy, my little laddie, dance to your daddy'... the final note is held as my opening solo is over, and other voices join mine. I listen carefully as we start to weave in harmony with each other, rising and falling in the familiar folk song, 'When the Boat Comes In'.

We've created our own version of two very well-known maritime songs, combining the traditional arrangement of 'When the Boat Comes In', with the reverential and stately music of the nautical hymn, 'Eternal Father'. Now it's the turn of the whole choir to take up the chorus. 'Eternal Father, strong to save / Whose arm hath bound the restless wave...'

As the voices soar around me, the lyrics resonate deeply within. At this moment, the power of those words, the true meaning of the cry: 'Oh hear us when we cry to Thee / For those in peril on the sea' hits me like a train.

Since losing Colin, there have been so many things I've simply had no choice but to get on with. Like anyone in my situation, I've taken a deep breath and simply took a step forwards, whatever the task was ahead. Music had always been my great passion, but for years after Colin's death, the one thing I was unable to do was sing.

I wanted to. I tried to. But each time, overwhelming grief would cause a tide of pain to rise up within me. You can hold down a lot of emotion if you have to. It's possible, even, to keep your feelings from showing in your voice as you go about your life. But with singing, the vocal comes from a deeper place inside. I'd be reduced to tears and sobs, the music opening the floodgates on the oceans of grief held within me.

And yet, here am I now, in full song.

Somehow, in seeking to repay those who helped me in my family's darkest hour, I realise, I've received a gift that I never expected. Surrounded by women who understand and, in too many cases, have suffered the same pain that I did, I know that I have found my voice once more. And, in doing so, I've found my path back to life.

I can't help feeling that in some way, being able to enjoy and participate in music again is Colin's final gift to me. And I am eternally indebted to my wonderful, lovely fisherman.

Thank you, my darling. My lovely man.

But I'd still trade every song I've ever sung to have you back again.

Blue Skies Ahead

August 1997

I wasn't looking for love when I moved back to Leigh-on-Sea, the Essex town where I'd grown up. After my marriage had broken down, I'd been living in Westcliff-on-Sea, just along the coast. But the landlord had decided to sell our flat, so I, a 31-year-old single mum, was trying to find somewhere for me and my two boys to live.

It was a real struggle. Leigh is a pretty little town looking out over the busy Thames Estuary. Even when the tide is out, leaving the boats leaning skew-whiff over the mudflats, the view can take your breath away: silver pools of water gleaming under a vast, pale sky, gulls wheeling and calling above. I'm not the only one who appreciates it, though: it's less than an hour on the train into London, so it attracts a lot of commuters too – City workers looking for somewhere a bit more quiet, so property prices can be pretty high.

As a single mum, money wasn't exactly plentiful, so there wasn't anything spare. The problem was that I was struggling to find a landlord who would take us without a month's rent as a deposit *and* a month's rent upfront. I was feeling desperate. I'd sold everything of value that I owned – including my guitars. I didn't have anything left, not even a mobile phone, so I used to have to run across the road to the local theatre near my flat, to use the public telephone.

I'd copy out numbers from the Yellow Pages and, when the boys were at school, would be standing for what felt like hours in this public telephone booth, phoning estate agents who looked after rentals in the area: 'Have you got anything? Anything at all?' But I wasn't getting anywhere. I felt like crying with frustration. And then I misdialled – phoning an agent whose number was listed above the one I'd meant to call.

'I'm really sorry,' he said. 'We don't do rentals.'

'Oh well,' I said. 'No chance of a lovely little cottage for a lone mum who's got to move soon?' – it was a long shot but what did I have to lose?

The voice on the other end of the phone laughed. 'Er, well, I might as it happens.'

My spirits leapt as he said, 'I've got to say, you've timed your call well, I'm just about to advertise my own place to let. Why don't you come down and see me? Say, about 2p.m. tomorrow?'

The terraced house was a little fisherman's cottage, he told me. Oh really, I wondered – maybe that's just a euphemism for tiny?

But this was a possible lifeline I had no intention of letting slip through my fingers. The following afternoon, I called into the estate agent's and he walked me round to see the cottage. I gasped when I saw it. A couple of hundred years old, it was beautiful, with roses growing up the brickwork – like something you'd see on a chocolate box.

I couldn't believe it. And the agent, Les, was absolutely lovely – what's more, his son was in the same class as my son Josh. He and his family were about to move out to house-sit a far larger property for a friend for a few years, which is why it was now available to rent, he explained. That was that. He did the deal for just a month's deposit, a sum that my parents were happy to lend me, and I signed on the dotted line.

Within the month, I'd moved in. I already knew Danielle, the girl next door, from the school playground. On the other side, an older gentleman was living there, Ken. The 'fisherman's cottage' tag wasn't just a bit of social history, I realised – Ken's family, the Dolbys, were an old fishing family who had lived there for years. Ken himself was just as I'd have thought a retired fisherman would look: kindly faced, a shock of white hair, a lovely smile, big, rough hands. Ken had lost his wife, I heard, and had a grown-up son. The first time I saw him was when I was moving in.

'Oi,' shouted Danielle, who was giving me a bit of a hand. 'This is our new neighbour, Jane.'

There he was: dark, stubbly, smiling.

'All right?' he said.

'Yes,' I said, 'nice to meet you' – but what I was really thinking was, oh, he stinks of fish. No wonder, because he'd just pulled up with a trailer full of them: bags and baskets of fish.

My boys and I settled in quickly. 'I'm just going next door to play with Colin,' my youngest, Henry, announced one day. I assumed this Colin was a little boy, perhaps Ken's grandson. It was only when Colin turned up on the doorstep to return him home that I realised it was the bloke I'd been fleetingly introduced to in the chaos of moving in. Henry, just seven years old, nonetheless identified Colin as a fascinating new friend.

You see, like his dad Ken, and Ken's dad before him, Colin was a fisherman. He didn't live next door, but he was a regular visitor to his dad's, keeping a workshop at the bottom of his garden where he maintained equipment for his boat. Henry soon got into the habit of going in the little alleyway between our houses to find him fixing nets, fitting a wheel, or busy at some other task that he found endlessly fascinating.

'Hello, Colin! Got any jobs for me?' he'd call, and Colin would gamely say, 'Oh yeah, I've got a really important job for you. You've got to burn that bit of string' – or something equally pointless, though Henry loved it. 'I've burnt that, I've burnt that, what else have I got to do?' I'd often find him sitting there in Ken's backyard 'helping' Colin, or just watching, talking.

Talking rather too much, it seemed. 'He really likes you, that man next door, he thinks you're beautiful,' Henry told me one day, in that matter-of-fact way kids have, before something else grabbed his attention. But it went on. Day after day he kept returning home, full of stories about how much Colin wanted to go out with me on a date. I have to say, I didn't take it as a compliment. My alarm bells went off. That Colin was telling a little boy this – I just thought it was weird, and said as much to Danielle my neighbour: 'I just think it's a bit creepy that he wants to hang out with a little kid.'

She wasn't having that. 'No, he's not weird, he's absolutely lovely,' she said. 'He's just shy, he's a really nice person.'

'Oh, well.' I sniffed. I wasn't convinced. But when I quietly asked around about the people next door, all my new neighbours said the same thing. The whole family was delightful, and Colin a lovely man with a gentle heart – many had known them since he was born. Even I, a born worrier, was reassured.

Still, over the next few days, as Henry continued to mention that Colin liked me, I thought, I'm going to have to tackle this. Scruffy clothes with a black woolly hat and smelling of fish? He just wasn't my type. I was very aware that I had to live next door to him, so I was keen to avoid any awkwardness.

So, one afternoon when I'd spotted him going into his dad's I went round – not all guns blazing, that's not my style at all – and asked for a quick word. He'd been kind to my little boy, and I didn't want to hurt his feelings.

'Look,' I said hurriedly, 'you're lovely with Henry, and you're a fantastic neighbour, but I want to tell you that I'm not in the market for a relationship.'

Having said my piece, I waited for Colin to defend himself, perhaps even apologise for putting me in this position.

Colin, it had to be said, did not seem quite as embarrassed as you might expect.

'What?' he said, seeming baffled.

'Well, I just want to tell you, you know, I don't want any bad feeling, I don't want any misunderstanding – after all, we've got to live next door to each other,' I waffled, wondering how much I'd have to say until he got the message.

'Well, I'm not really looking for a relationship,' he replied politely.

For once, I had nothing to say. 'But Henry told me ...' I flapped, just as Colin said, 'Well, Henry has told me ...' And then it all came out.

When Henry had been coming back to me saying, 'Oh, Colin thinks you're lovely,' he'd been trotting off next door to tell Colin some sweet nothings from 'me' in return, I learnt. My little boy, we realised, had taken it upon himself to act as a would-be Cupid.

Colin started laughing – really laughing. 'What a bloody cheek!' he said, wiping tears from his eyes. 'Your son has been telling me for two months how much you fancy me! He's said all the same things to me!'

And Henry had not always been that flattering, I learnt.

'You know, my mum's quite fat,' my seven-year-old had remarked to Colin one day. 'Well, she really loves eating: why don't you take her out for dinner?'

What Colin was too kind to tell me then – but Henry admitted later – is that my little boy had said whatever he could think of to make his new friend want to go out with

8

me. Including, to my horror, that I was 'lying on my bed with my top off and all my boobies out'! How many did he think I had? I cringed.

'Henry,' Colin had responded. 'I don't think you should be saying these kinds of things to me, mate.' It was just mortifying, the whole thing.

Though Colin kept back the worst of it that day, I felt my face growing red. But I couldn't help it – I started laughing, too. I'm always ready to see the funny side of things, and this did tickle me. Of course, given how well I know Colin now, I realise it would never have crossed his mind to say anything out of line to a child. Nor did he have any burning wish to hang out with a kid all the time. He didn't say it outright, but it was clear it was just my son popping round whenever he felt like it, and Colin being so kind that he didn't want to turn him away.

Even back then, I could see I had got this man wrong. The best thing for it would be to move onto a new footing, I decided, clear the air and keep things neighbourly.

'Well, we've established it's all nonsense,' I said, my smile still lingering as our laughter subsided.

'Yeah, yeah,' he said quickly, looking away. 'It's all nonsense.'

But you know, don't you? It's the way someone looks at you, and acts around you. And while I realised that Henry had been embellishing what Colin had said, there had been a kernel of truth in the messages he'd been relaying to me.

When my son had been telling me, 'Oh, Colin thinks you're lovely,' Colin *had* said those things, even if Leigh's very own Cupid had given him a bit of a prompt: 'Do you think my mum's pretty?' 'Oh yeah, she's gorgeous, aren't you lucky having a lovely mum like that.'

And then Henry had been encouraging it all with my totally made-up responses: 'My mum would love you to take her out for dinner,' and the rest!

So, while my little boy have taken it upon himself to try to bring us together, I could tell that by drawing a line between us in the way I had, I was putting in place something that Colin would agree to – and he was very respectful of what I wanted – but wasn't his choice.

At the same time, our chat shifted things for me. You know when someone puts an idea in your head, and you start thinking about someone quite differently? That was what it felt like for me. Once the idea was out there, there was a sort of power to it. Having said this thing – 'Oh, I'm not interested in a relationship' – somehow made the whole idea of a relationship something tangible. So that was when it all got a bit awkward, and we stopped being so natural with each other for a while. We'd see each other, going in and out of our front doors, but it'd just be a nod and a quick hello.

At the time, I was still working in a pub for a couple of hours a day, but because it was a few bus rides away, it was a time-consuming journey there and back. With the boys to look after – Henry and his elder brother Josh, then aged eleven – I was pretty busy. I would just see Colin as neighbours do. Yet, as the weeks passed, he started to let me know he felt another way.

In my little fisherman's cottage I had a real wood fire, which demanded constant feeding when winter drew in. Money was always tight, so the kids and I would go for walks in the woods to gather kindling, and if I managed to get a log back – I didn't have a car – I'd be out at the back afterwards, trying to saw it up. There was quite a lot of work involved in keeping that thing going, however picturesque it was. Then one Friday, after we'd been living at the cottage for several months, I opened the back door and stopped dead. There was this pile of logs, all neatly sawn and stacked up. Beep went my phone – a text message from Colin, saying: 'Hope you all keep warm this weekend.' Another time, I realised the boys' broken bikes had been quietly mended, without him saying a word.

That wasn't all. Early one frosty morning, I had quite a shock as I looked out of the kitchen window, sipping my coffee. There was this bloke in working clothes – a bright orange boiler suit, steel-capped boots – standing in front of a set of football nets which looked, I noticed, suspiciously like the fishing nets I'd seen on the back of Colin's van. 'For the boys!' he was calling, waving happily from the middle of all this.

Josh, I remembered, had made a throwaway comment the other day about how he'd like to play football – and this was the result. Colin had been there for ages, putting this football net together, hanging it from goalposts; just three-quarters the size of a normal goal, it was huge.

Colin must have noticed my bemused expression. I'd not imagined seeing a man in a bright orange boiler suit, building goalposts, into my usual 'things-to-expect-in-the-morning' routine.

He just grinned at me through the window, stuck his thumbs up. 'Do you think they'll like it?' he shouted, his breath visible in the chilly air, and then disappeared out of sight.

The boys tumbled outside in their dressing gowns, me following, to inspect the new equipment. The kids, of course, were thrilled. And what about me? Secretly, so was I. Despite the cold outside, I was aware of a growing warmth. People can say a lot of things, but when they *do* things – it's quite potent. Actions really do speak louder than words, and can erode quite a lot of resistance. These quiet, yet loving surprises were making me start – very gradually – to think about how kind Colin was.

He even helped me out when my plumbing broke. One day, the toilet just came away from the wall – water was gushing everywhere. 'Please go and get Colin,' I told Henry as I reached for old towels and buckets. It was simply my first thought: he'd help me out.

Within a few minutes, Henry trotted back up the stairs with Colin in tow.

'Look, I'm really, really sorry,' I told him, 'but as you can see, I'm having a turd catastrophe!'

Colin laughed and laughed – and just got on with it.

'You go back to the workshop,' he told Henry, giving him a list of tools, while he settled down on the floor by my side to help me stem the tide. Henry, proud to be helping, rushed off.

'Maybe if you didn't have such a lardy arse you wouldn't be in this situation,' Colin joked.

'Oh, thanks very much!' I said, feigning indignation but in truth, very much starting to laugh too.

Before I knew it, the job was done.

'Thanks, Colin, I really appreciate it,' I said, as I saw him out of the front door.

'Oh, no bother,' he said, giving me a smile as he headed off.

Then, a few weeks after that first conversation about our feelings, we ran into each other again, as we often did going in and out. This time we both felt a bit less awkward, and we ended up having a proper chat: how are you doing, what have you been up to, that sort of thing. And then we moved on to Henry, and some of the things he'd said while busy playing Cupid.

'God, wasn't he just...' Colin had started.

'Yes,' I said. 'What an imagination!'

And that was the moment he said it – 'Well, in my case, it's true' – just straight out, like that.

'Oh right, okay, jolly good,' I replied, flustered, resisting the overwhelming urge to wring my hands in embarrassment. Instead I changed the subject: 'Well, I'd better get on, I've the boys' tea to make, things to do.'

I didn't know how to respond. Colin's unexpected declaration left me feeling incredibly awkward and I prayed he had no further similar announcements planned. Thankfully, he didn't say another word on the subject but it didn't matter – it was too late, the truth was out there: he had feelings for me. Bloody hell. What on earth was I supposed to do with that snippet of information?

There was another incident too, that – in retrospect – would take on a different light. That spring, it was my friend Wendy's fortieth birthday. It was a riotous night – lots of musicians there, all my usual crowd, and the celebrations went on till about four o'clock in the morning. I'd just sat down for a quick break from the festivities, when I checked my phone out of habit.

I had about five or six missed calls: all from Colin.

I frowned. 'You know,' I said to my friend Phil, a local musician, 'this is really bloody freaky that he's phoning me at two o' clock in the morning. It's weirding me out.'

'If you were in love with him,' said Phil, with a wry smile, 'you'd think it was the most romantic thing in the world.'

'But I'm *not* in love with him, so it's all actually just a bit creepy really, don't you think?'

'Not really,' said Phil most unhelpfully.

And when I next saw Colin, I told him as much outright. 'Look, Colin, why did you call me so many times? I didn't like it. It felt like you were really on my case. I felt a bit cornered.'

'Oh, right,' he said. 'Sorry about that.'

I couldn't read his expression. 'What were you ringing me about anyway?'

He shrugged. 'Oh, I was up early for work. I knew you were at this party, so . . .' His words tailed off. So he didn't really explain – and I didn't press any further. I was just pleased a line had been drawn under the incident and I'd set some boundaries.

You see, I'd been on my own for a long time when I met Colin. It's always lovely to have that intimacy, and that love, but not at any cost. It's got to be the right person. I've always felt like that, I've never felt desperate for a man. Colin was kind and he was lovely – and it was quite obvious how he felt about me now.

But I knew that I didn't feel quite the same way about him – not yet.

A New Dawn

We're not really used to seeing our lives take a new path. More often, we don't notice the subtle sign-posts – the significance of a decision, the implications of a choice – until we're looking back. But the day I went out with Colin on his boat was different. It changed everything.

Like everybody, I was intrigued by him being a fisher-man. As I'd learn, whenever he told anyone – at a party, or wherever – it was all anyone would talk about. They'd stop conversations to pepper him with questions: 'What do you catch? What, in Southend? Where do you go in the river then?'

We may be an island nation, but somehow we've become so removed from this industry, this way of life, that people were just delighted to find that here was a real live fisher-man, right in front of them – and I was no different, always asking him questions. Colin was a sixth-generation fisherman – and, I thought, likely more than that. 'There's saltwater in my blood,' his father, Ken, once told me. He explained that the Dolbys had been fishing for at least three hundred years: they'd traced themselves as far back as 1780, to a fisherman called Samuel Dolby.

Colin caught cod, Dover sole, even lobster – whatever

was swimming out there in the Thames Estuary, with him sometimes travelling a 20-mile round trip in a day.

'I go up the coast as far as Clacton,' he told me, 'or even out east to the edge of the North Sea. But no further, as my boat's not big enough for those waves.'

It fascinated me, and I said so.

'Well, you can always come out on the boat sometime,' he said.

'Yeah, yeah,' I'd say, 'I'd have to get organised, sort out childcare.'

But then, one weekend that March, my first spring in the cottage, I did, while the boys were away. Could I go?

'Of course you can,' he said. 'The blossom is on the trees so the soles are back in the river.'

I was simply looking forward to a day out on the water. Despite growing up on the Essex coast, it was all new to me. The sea had been, quite literally, the backdrop to our lives in Leigh. I didn't know any fishermen, and I'd never considered going out on a fishing boat; the closest I had got was a barge trip on the Norfolk Broads with my parents! Still, I felt drawn to the sea. Even when I was a kid, I loved the water. I was completely comfortable in Colin's company and just thought it would be an interesting thing to do. And it was – magical, in fact.

But fishing's not glamorous, that's for sure. I was wrapped up in layers of proper clothing, jeans, jumpers, a coat, for a start. It's always cold on the water; even if it's baking on land, it's never as hot out on the sea. I might have put on a bit of make-up, though, and run a brush through my hair, but that was about the extent of it. I've never been a heels and blow-dry sort of girl – I'm not really that concerned with my appearance.

Colin, as most fishermen do, always wore the same thing: jeans, the fisherman's uniform, with the checked shirt; those heavy boots, like builders wear; and then the smocks – chunky blue jumpers with the two little pockets at the front, where they put their gutting knives and bits and pieces. The smocks just go over everything, as protection.

We had to set off really early, about two o'clock in the morning, because of the timing of the tides. That was nothing special: Colin would often have to be up and out at one, two, three o'clock, I knew. And so, through the dark town, he drove me the short way to Two Tree Island, a wild patch of grassland and birds' nests reached by bridge from Leigh-on-Sea's old town down by the seafront. As we crossed the little bridge in his battered blue Ford Orion, the darkness deepened – the final stretch of road down to Two Tree was completely unlit.

'I've never been down here at night, it looks completely different,' I said.

'Don't worry, love,' Colin gave me a reassuring wink. 'I know this road like the back of my hand, I could drive down here with my eyes closed.'

I smiled back at him. 'You know,' I said with a laugh, teasing him, 'I bet I know the real reason you like coming to Two Tree ... I'm told they do a lot of dogging round here.'

'Oh no,' said Colin seriously. 'I don't think many people

would walk their dogs this late at night. It's far too dark!'
He honestly didn't know what I was talking about.

'Er, no . . . not that sort of dogging, Colin.'

But I decided to leave it at that. There was an innocence
to him that I warmed to.

From Two Tree, it was his usual routine: take his little
dinghy out to his skiff, which was a boat big enough to
get us out to his 40-foot trawler, moored still further out.
Yes, that's three boats: it's because the water's so shallow
near to the land. The bigger boats have to wind their way
through 'guts' under the surface – these channels forking
through the mudflats – that they can sail along. You can see
them when the tides go out. But some boats, the bigger
vessels, just can't ever come in that close.

As we reached the causeway, with its rows of little dinghies resting among the scrubby grasses, Colin jumped out
and started preparing his own dinghy for the water. Getting
out of the car to watch him, I couldn't believe the pace
at which he worked. He darted about, grabbing oars and
kit and pushing the dinghy the last few feet into the black
water, then passed me a frayed nylon rope with one end
fastened to the little wooden boat.

'Hold the rope, will you darlin', I'll be back in a mo',
don't let go.'

'I won't,' I said.

There I stood in the moonlight, holding the rope and
listening to the water gently lapping as Colin climbed back
into the car. At breakneck speed, he went into a rapid three-
point turn to park the car, taking it right to the water's

edge. Then he ran back down to me and climbed into the dinghy, not even out of breath.

'Hand me the oars, would you, and the diesel can' – hastily, I followed my instructions. Then Colin held out his hands and I stepped awkwardly from the causeway into the dinghy, the wood under my feet moving with the waves. His hands were big and rough from years of hard outdoor work – but they felt safe.

'Just sit down there,' he said, 'in the middle.'

The splash of oars broke the still night as he started rowing across the water for the couple of minutes it took to reach his skiff. I was enchanted: everything looked so beautiful and strange under the silver light. We fell quiet, as Colin rowed – we were moving quickly, and he was working hard – but every so often our eyes would meet. I'd smile and look away, aware that he was holding his gaze for just that beat longer than was necessary.

The spell was broken as we reached Colin's skiff – the bigger boat that would carry us and his gear out to his trawler, which was moored by Southend pier. As we motored the final stretch over the water, she emerged out of the night: blue below, and white on top. I mouthed the name written on her side in a looping blue script: *Louisa*. She was bigger than I expected, a hefty presence, and covered in – to my eyes – mysterious cables and ropes and rigging.

Once we'd climbed aboard, he was a different person. As he moved about the boat, pulling ropes and moving kit, it was like seeing a cumbersome old seal, shuffling about on land, suddenly flashing about in the water, a creature of grace and power. I saw a side to him that I didn't see on land, in everyday life.

I started to fire questions at him: How did you get into it? Is this your boat? And, as he worked, he talked me through what he was doing. 'I started off working for my dad, as crew,' he explained, 'lots of fishermen start that way. But when friends of the family had a boat free that I could skipper, it meant I could go off and run my own operation.' And being a skipper on that boat had allowed him to earn enough money to buy the one we were on: the *Louisa*.

As I looked out into the cold night, the water seemed so quiet; but something occurred to me. I knew the river was a channel for ferries, which could cause massive swells. You'd notice them from the shore sometimes. 'What happens if another boat comes along?' I asked.

'They can knock you sideways, if the boat's not positioned right. And, of course, if you've moved into the shipping lane, you've got to stay alert.' He didn't talk himself up, but it was very clear to me that fishing was a man's job. You can't be a boy and do it; you have to be incredibly strong, physically and mentally. You've got to keep your wits about you, be ready to react to changes in the weather or to any 'big ones' – waves – that might come along.

As for the fish, he caught them by trawling – dragging nets along the bottom of the Thames Estuary. Dover sole, his main catch, are flatfish, so that's where they live. When the boat is going along it's called 'steaming' and you can effectively set an autopilot. While that was happening, Colin would be busy gutting all the fish he'd already hauled up, because by the time they go to market, to the fish merchants, they've got to be gutted, washed and ready – each single one. He could gut hundreds an hour.

It's brutal work, definitely, but there was a beauty to it as well, I noticed: the rhythm of picking up a fish, the flash of the knife, a flick of the hand and the guts are in the air, the gulls darting down to grab them before they even hit the water. And as Colin said, 'It's nature, it's not like the fish have kept in a battery farm.' Colin, it struck me, really understood nature in a way that most of us don't any more. 'Oh, I don't need all that navigational gear,' he said at one point. 'I can navigate the old way, by the stars.' And without any self-consciousness about it, he was very much a part of the natural world himself.

And, all the time, as he worked, we kept talking – about his work, my kids, our hopes and dreams, past relationships. 'There's no point regretting things,' Colin said – but I sensed that here was a man who was ready for a different stage of his life: for love, a family. 'You can use a situation as a sort of trampoline for a better situation,' he said. 'It's about turning whatever you are, and wherever you're at, into where you want to be.' As we chatted, I felt very safe and comfortable with him. He was so easy to be with on a one-to-one level. At the same time, watching him in his element, moving about his boat, so capable, so strong, I felt that unmistakable electricity – almost a current between us – too.

Out on the waves, moving with the water, I felt blissfully

calm. Turning to view the land from the sea, I remembered Neil Armstrong's thoughts on the perspective, as an astronaut, from space: 'It suddenly struck me that that tiny pea, pretty and blue, was the Earth. I put up my thumb and shut one eye, and my thumb blotted out the planet Earth. I didn't feel like a giant. I felt very, very small.' Sitting there, I knew some of what he meant. I felt as though my soul had been nourished: the madness of the world simply lifted from my mind.

As the sun rose, it lit the water, leaving us alone in a glorious, glowing world – and, as I watched Colin against the changing sky, that movement from darkness into light felt like a metaphor for my feelings as well. For, suddenly, I absolutely knew, with the most profound conviction, that I would marry him. I looked at him and felt that stomach-churning euphoria – you know, that falling-in-love feeling – and thought, oh my God, you are just lovely.

It was like something clicking together. At the time, although I was just into my thirties, I was feeling long in the tooth: two kids, a failed marriage, a couple of other road-to-nowhere relationships under my belt. I'd definitely been in love before; and I'd had all the other stuff associated with that – the excitement – but after that was gone, there wasn't the substance there. But this was totally different – it was inexplicable. This was a certainty that I'd be safe with him, that he'd take care of me, that there'd be no games. He was just this beautiful person – a good, good person. I knew that I'd finally found the man whom I would be with, whom I would marry, who was right for me.

Sitting on that deck, watching him work, talking about our lives, relationships, the children, I felt like I was being swept out on a great tide of hope. It's quite a grind, doing things on your own, and Colin – he just made everything feel easy. He'd always say, 'Nothing's a problem, unless you make it a problem.' He was a very positive influence.

And for me, that event – I don't know what else I can call it – of moving from one emotional state to another was mirrored by the rising of the sun, and the ending of the darkness.

I didn't know, back then, how powerful that imagery would one day become for me. 'It's always darkest just before the dawn' was a phrase I'd later cling to for hope, longing to see a chink of light in the blackness. But then, I was just lost in the happiness of the moment.

The weird thing is, when I look back I get those emotions again and Colin's not here, but I can remember them so clearly that my body still feels them. I fell completely in love with him in that moment. And then he kissed me, on the boat, under the rising sun.

Out of my Depth

It certainly wasn't all sunshine and romance, though, as I sat on the deck that day. The *Louisa* was a working boat, and there was no chance of me forgetting that. The hold stank of diesel, and you'd get very sick if you spent much time bobbing around in there – I learnt that quickly!

Then there was the fishing itself to get used to. When Colin lifted the nets out of the water on the winch, they'd come out dripping, a sort of upside-down triangular mass; then he'd pull apart the bit at the bottom, called the cod end, to release the fish he'd caught onto the deck in a huge, silver, living mass. There were so many, so deep, that they were piling against the sides of the boat, all moving and twisting. And that was a shock to me – a proper shock. I felt incredibly uncomfortable about seeing these hundreds of creatures dying; I didn't like that at all. Of course, I knew what a fisherman does, but the reality of it was brutal. Not to mention I was a vegetarian when I met Colin.

The reason I didn't eat meat – or fish – wasn't because I thought human beings shouldn't eat animals, but because I really had an issue with the farming methods involved: how the animals that we eat live. The difficulty was I couldn't afford to buy free-range, organic meat, where I could be confident they'd had a decent life, so I just didn't eat meat at all. But when I was out on the boat it was a primal thing. A hunt. An honesty. It reminded me of when an animal is in its natural environment: the prey enjoys a completely normal existence until the point of capture and consumption. An animal just catches an animal and eats it. And that reminded me of fishing: those fish were not farmed, they had totally natural lives until they were caught, then eaten. So that's why I started eating fish again, eventually, but for a long time I couldn't.

And it's not just fish that gets hauled out of the water: it's cod, Dover sole, yes, but also things you'd hope weren't being flushed out to sea – plastic bags, sanitary towels, condoms! It was a real eye-opener for me, how we abuse nature's bounty. But while he kept on working, I was just sitting out on the seas, talking to Colin, for 12 hours. That's quite rare in life today, to have the opportunity to talk and talk, with no one else around, for a whole day.

And I got to know him. Yes, he looked like a scruffy old fisherman – because he was! Even a bit piratical, with his earring. But there was so much more to him than that. He had a caustic sense of humour: he'd make me roar with laughter with this very dark wit. And he was really smart, in a way that had nothing to do with textbooks.

I was wary: I wasn't looking for love. By the time I was 25, I was a divorced single parent of two little boys – which is young, I know. I'd been married a year to a musician I'd met when we'd been in the same band – it's a heady atmosphere, creating something together. But neither of us was very emotionally grown-up and, as we'd discover, we weren't really ready for it all. 'You don't realise it at the time, of course,' I told Colin. 'I remember being pregnant with my first baby, Josh, and saying, "Oh, it won't change anything, I'll still travel, do everything I plan." I was so naïve.'

Aren't we all, though, when we're young and green? Growing up in Leigh, all I'd cared about was music: I'd get letters home for singing in class. So I didn't even finish my education, leaving my girls' school at 15 without any O levels. I worked in a hairdresser's, until I left that – to much parental fretting – to sell sandwiches. I'd told my long-suffering parents I was going to be a pop star anyway, so it didn't matter. I must admit I'd not actually figured out how I was going to make the transition from sandwich seller to successful singer – but I never let life get in the way of a dream! In the meantime, I had itchy feet. As soon as I was 18 I hit the old hippy trail, living all over: Devon, Yorkshire, but I spent most time in Bristol. I simply went to stay with a friend there and never came back. I ended up in a sort of commune – a large shared house in Portishead – where I learnt to play the guitar, something I'd always wanted to do, and kept myself afloat working in bars.

But no one can stay Peter Pan for ever and once I became a mum, things had to change. It was time to be responsible. I could never have predicted how much it was possible to love a child and nothing mattered more than providing security and a future for my gorgeous baby. I came back to Leigh for a more settled existence – in my own fashion. I'd take the boys to school and go and stand in Southend high street with my guitar, busking from half past nine to half past two, while the boys were at school. What a life! Of course, it was becoming obvious to me that my teenage dreams of musical stardom weren't enough to feed a family. I didn't like performing live at all; if I played a gig with the bands I'd fall in and out of, I'd suffer from paralysing stage fright, to the point where I'd be locked in the toilet shaking and being sick simply overwhelmed with panic and fear. There was absolutely nothing I enjoyed about being in front of an audience: I felt like a fraud, like someone was just going to come up to me and say, 'Who do you think you are, doing this?' I also worried constantly about forgetting the words and letting the rest of the band down. I loved singing and could just about cope with busking as people just walked past me, I definitely felt more comfortable warbling away in the privacy of my own home than on a stage.

The penny finally dropped – I was not destined for a career on the stage. I was at peace with this realisation. It felt right.

So I took myself back into education. In the death throes of my marriage, a friend told me about something called an access course run by the local college, which opened my eyes. I had the most inspiring tutor who would go on to become one of my dearest friends. For me, the access course was a second chance – a year of intensive education that allowed me to apply for a degree course at university, which I did.

When my marriage broke up I moved to nearby Westcliff with the children and continued my education. When I wasn't in classes, I worked in a burger bar on the High Street, doing shifts to ensure I could make the afternoon school run.

By the time I met Colin, I'd done two years of my degree, which included some youth work with young offenders. But it got to the point where it was difficult to afford rent, fares and childcare on a student budget; and keeping a roof over our heads took priority. I thought the best solution was to defer for a while and continue my studies at another time, when my circumstances were a bit better, but life has a habit of getting in the way of the very best of plans, so I didn't finish my degree. I threw myself into being the best mother I could and I loved being a mum. The boys were my everything. I used to go to church and house groups so most of my socialising revolved around church activities and the people there – my world was quite small really. But I was very happy.

And so my story poured out. Colin was a good listener, just easy to talk to. I got a sense that he was a very peaceful person in every way: he liked candlelight, he liked the woods, being on the beach. A sixth-generation fisherman, he had been on boats since he was four years old, helping out his dad and his grandad. 'I couldn't do anything else,' he said, 'I was born to do it.'

And what he loved about it, I could tell, had become such a part of who he was. Fishing really is a way of life, it's not a nine-to-five and you switch off afterwards. It shapes who you are. There's no coasting through an afternoon slumped at your desk with a cup of tea, taking it easy. Out there among the waves and the spray, you are battling with exhaustion, battling with fear, battling with the total disappointment of being out all day and coming back with nothing. It's a job that trains you to keep your eye on the prize, play the long game. And when you do find a good spot for fish, haul in a full net, bring the boat safely home, there's enjoyment and pride in actually seeing something through. It builds you up.

Still, some of it can't be reduced to box-ticking qualities that recruiters would like. There's something else out there. As a fisherman said to me once, 'The sea is one of our last great freedoms.' And that does something to a personality, spending all that time riding the waves, just a speck on this expanse of wild water.

So Colin was very in tune with nature, but he was also incredibly intuitive with people: despite spending so much time alone, he knew when to bring something up, when not to; when to move in and out of a situation. He was just operating on a very natural frequency. He was, I guessed, inexperienced with women – I think he'd had a couple of girlfriends, but nothing serious – and yet even that day on the boat it struck me that he was quite emotionally insightful. I didn't know how, him having so little contact with so few people. But he just knew how to be with people and – as I'd find out – he knew how to love a person.

Maybe, I wonder now, he hadn't had his heart broken and maybe that was why he could be vulnerable. Maybe he didn't even realise that's what he was doing. And, under-lying it all, even later in the day when I was getting tired, was that heady, lovely feeling: the best way to describe it is when you're standing near someone you like and you're almost touching hands, but hold back. When you've got that awareness of their every movement, their closeness – and it's almost hard to breathe. That was us – on the edge of something big.

Finally, we headed into Colin's mooring, near the pier, and I watched him deftly unload all the fish in plastic baskets into the skiff, then from the skiff to the dinghy, from the dinghy to the trailer attached to his Land Rover. It was hard physical work. Off we went, then, with a trailer full of fish to the fish merchant in Hadleigh – to drop off the catch. The boats use ice to keep the fish fresh on long trips, but Colin stayed relatively local, so they just had to go straight to the fish merchant he sold to. We walked into a chilly warehouse full of big fridges and polystyrene boxes, where the catch would be weighed, then stored.

Colin would leave a 'fish ticket', he explained, listing the name of his boat and how much he'd caught, as a record, and go and get paid at the end of the week. It would end up at London's famous Billingsgate fish market, or maybe the local fisherman's co-operative, maybe the local fishmonger's, before it reached its final destination on someone's plate at a restaurant or home. That done, we went to see his dad Ken and had a cup of tea. After a day on the waves I was exhausted by that point, but buzzing too: I just didn't want to be away from him. Finally, he took me home and then the boys came back, and the usual bustle of day-to-day life took over again.

And that was my baptism into commercial fishing – a foreign yet fascinating world to me. It didn't cross my mind that it might be a dangerous world, too. I was floating on happiness, and life seemed so full of light and laughter. For if, on the surface, everything was the same, underneath everything had changed. Because I just couldn't stop thinking about Colin. It was sole season then, I remember, March time. Blossom on the trees, and love blossoming in my heart too – those few weeks from the end of winter to the beginning of spring.

Friction Makes the Pearl

The next day, Colin was meant to go to work but he couldn't, because the weather was too bad to go out on his boat – gusty, with rain clouds brewing.

'Fancy coming along to the marina with me?' he said. 'I've some jobs to do, but we can have a sandwich and a pint.'

With the boys at friends' houses for tea, I jumped at the chance to spend more time with him.

As we drove there, I felt the same current between us. Oh no, oh no, I thought, my stomach turning over. I'm really going to fall in love with him – and there's nothing I can do about it. It was the inevitability of it all that scared me. On the surface, though, it was all still quite casual.

After Colin picked up a few things for his boat, we headed to the café, tucked in a corner of the marina. I went to the toilet and when I came back there he was as I'd left him – except he was wearing, calm as you please, a curly bright blue wig.

Now, earlier I'd noticed that behind the bar there was a polystyrene head with a really curly bright blue wig, left over from some fancy dress event at the marina a few days before. Colin must have said to the barman, 'Oh, lend us that for a minute, I'm going to surprise my friend.'

Well, surprise was one word for it I suppose.

'Please take it off,' I muttered under my breath as I sat down. 'It's a bit embarrassing.'

'Nope,' he said, shaking his head. 'You know, I'm really starting to love this new look actually!'

'Colin, please take it off. You look like a nutter!' But he wouldn't budge.

'Your trouble is you've got no sense of style.' He winked at me and leant back in his chair. 'A bit longer hanging around with me will soon sort that out though.'

If, the day before, I'd got to know this masculine man on a boat, I was now seeing Colin's other side – the fun-loving side that just didn't worry what other people thought of him. He was really enjoying seeing me cringe – and didn't mind looking a total idiot just to achieve that.

It's no good being pissed off with him, he's not going to take it off, I thought – and, finally, started laughing. It was one of those make-or-break moments, but that's why he was good for me – I was learning not to take myself so seriously.

And in the days that followed, we kept seeing each other. When you fancy someone you look for excuses to see them, don't you? There'd be a knock on the door, and it would be Colin. 'I've brought you some fish,' he'd say, handing me a bag of freshly caught sole. Or, 'I've brought you a lobster.'

'Oh thanks!' I'd say, startled and smiling – thinking, now, I wonder how I'm going to cook that?

Colin told me that I was the one for him quite soon after that first day on the boat together.

Typically, he didn't mince his words. 'I'm not messing about now,' was how he phrased it, quite gruffly. 'Come on, girl!'

'No,' I said, thoughtfully. 'No, nor am I.'

It was just as if we both thought: this is it then.

But despite my initial certainty, in the weeks and days after that moment of clarity on the boat I sometimes worried that the differences between Colin and me would prove too great. He was so different from what I was used to, or had imagined for myself. All those artists, poets and musicians out there, and I'm falling for a fisherman!

When the kids were in bed, and I had time to think, my mind would start turning. Admit it, I'd think to myself, no one would have expected us to make a couple. My world was one of music, smoky pubs, late night curries and after-hours sing-a-longs. Yes, I was a mum, and I'd had to face up to my responsibilities, but in some ways I still lived a Peter Pan existence: friends with a crowd of never-grow-olds who dreamt of musical success into middle age and beyond. My fisherman, meanwhile, was busy working with the day-to-day realities of life – for what, really, is more real than feeding ourselves? He belonged to our last hunter-gatherer tradition, I'd think, one of modern life's few links with our wilder past. Our worlds didn't really collide, I'd think to myself, so much as never actually come into contact!

I'd mull, too, the twist of fate that had brought me to him. Colin, for instance, just wasn't a pub person, so there would have been no chance of us meeting, say, on a night out. Even if he had been in a pub, he would never have known how to approach a woman. He was a solitary person, and he was shy. He would have thought, oh, I wouldn't want to make her feel uncomfortable. I could give you a million reasons why it wouldn't have worked very well, him picking up a girl in that environment. Colin thought love had passed him by. Meeting me, the way he did, would have been the only way he met somebody, really. That's why I was so lucky to live next door to him – I doubt I'd ever have met him otherwise.

And yet. The pull to him was so strong. Over the weeks, so, so gradually, almost without my realising, the distance between our worlds seemed to matter less and less. I was just aware of this new feeling of happiness – everything felt so much lighter with him in my life. It was as if the sun had come out after a tough winter: I had that extra spring in my step, a smile on my face.

One day, it struck me: our differences meant we complemented each other. Whereas my default position was to analyse everything to death, he didn't navel-gaze: he just got on with things. For me, that was a total change of pace. I'd only ever been out with musicians and writers – arty types, you know – and they're all so bloody complicated and often extremely self-absorbed. And, I'll admit, I was erring a bit on complicated myself: listening to answerphone messages thinking, 'Does he mean this, or does he mean that?' Eventually, you just want someone to be clear and not play a game. In Colin, I found just that.

Really, he was a breath of fresh air. When Colin said, 'I'll be round at eight o'clock,' he was round at eight o'clock. He never, ever left me in a state of having to invent excuses for why he might be late, or why he might not be there: 'Oh, he probably hasn't rung because of so-and-so.' If Colin said he'd ring, he'd ring. If he said he'd do something, regardless of what had happened or how he felt, he'd do it. He was manly in the real sense of manly – emotionally mature. No amount of my own terrible timekeeping would cause him to behave in a way that was less than he expected from himself, even if my inability to be on time did drive him nuts! He said everyone else had their watch set to Greenwich Mean Time but mine was set to 'Planet Jane Time'. In the ever-changing world I inhabited, he became my anchor in every way.

There were so many occasions when he showed me I could rely on him, but one episode really sums him up. I was expecting him round one day, but – unbeknown to me – his car had broken down in Thorpe Bay, which is just along the coast from Leigh. But instead of phoning me and telling me this, he caught the train from Thorpe Bay to Leigh-on-Sea so he could run up the hill to me. He'd said he would come, so he was going to come – that was how his mind worked. There was no reason to ring and start telling me about his car troubles, as he saw it.

And he had quite a time getting to me! 'When I got to Thorpe Bay,' he told me later, with some bemusement, 'I couldn't figure out how to operate the ticket machine at the station.' What? It turned out that, while he'd been on a train before – he used to go and watch West Ham play when he was little – he had only ever paid over the counter. Since he'd started driving, he'd had no reason to repeat the experience, which meant he had no idea what to do with all the machines and turnstiles.

That was typical of Colin. You know, you meet people and you say, did you used to watch so-and-so on the telly when you were a kid? 'No' – totally blank. He had no terms of reference in that way. The reason was quite simply that his family didn't watch telly; they were out on the boat. Not all fishermen are like that, by any means, but his family was very traditional. I think they even had a tin bath when Colin was a kid. When I met him, he hadn't ever used a hole-in-the-wall cash machine. In fact, getting to know him was almost like meeting somebody from another planet, in that it felt as if he had just been put here. He was sort of untainted by the world – really untouched. He hadn't bought into any advertising myths, any 'You should wear this, or that'. He was totally free within his own mind. It was incredible.

I don't want to give the impression he was in a dream world, though – quite the opposite. Colin was incredibly practical and resourceful. Give him a few bits of cardboard and a bit of string and he'd make a radio, I'd joke. If something went wrong with his car, it wouldn't cross his mind to go to a garage, he'd go to his mate Alan's scrapyard, fish around till he'd found something and then stay and have a chat and a cup of tea. I've no idea what they'd talk about – scrap, fish, who knows?

More than anything, what drew me to him was that he was a real man. A real man who was confident and assured enough in his own masculinity that he wasn't afraid to be vulnerable.

'Remember that night I got all those missed calls from you?' I asked him once, thinking of Wendy's birthday party. 'What was that all about?'

He gave me a look. 'You hurt my feelings when you said I was making you feel cornered. I just wanted to tell you I couldn't stop thinking about you.'

And of course when he told me that – and I *was* falling completely in love with him – I realised my friend Phil had been right. It *is* lovely, when someone knows you're still up, to call just to tell you you're on his mind: 'I know you're at a party but I can't stop thinking about you.'

Oh, he wasn't perfect. He liked some terrible music. I did work very hard on introducing him to Joni Mitchell, James Taylor, Neil Young, all my favourites. Once I even switched on the cassette player in his car and what did I hear but Chas and Dave! Kidding myself that I was something of a music connoisseur, I tried to sell it to myself: 'Right, this is world music, this is indigenous cockney music!' But it was never music I'd choose to play. He did absolutely love James Taylor and Cat Stevens. He also liked peaceful music, like Enya.

Likewise, we had completely different taste in films. We went to see *Eyes Wide Shut* once, starring Tom Cruise and Nicole Kidman, which I didn't really enjoy at all. Even so, I like to come out of a film and talk about the storyline, the acting, what did we think, was so-and-so believable – all that sort of stuff, to pick it apart a bit.

'What did you think of the film then?' I asked as we left the cinema, eager to talk about the characters, the plot, the acting.

'I quite liked that car,' was his verdict – referring to what Tom Cruise was driving in the film.

I persevered. 'But what do you think of Nicole Kidman's acting? I wasn't sure she was totally convincing as that character . . .' I was ready for a big discussion of her style and talent.

'Well,' he said, 'if you don't like her acting, don't go and see any more of her films.'

I used to get so frustrated, I'd think, I'm not going anywhere with you again!

And, as with all couples, there'd be occasional disagreements. I came to realise later that often it's the friction that creates the pearl.

One day, we were sitting talking about what we'd do if we won the lottery.

'What would *you* do,' I said, 'if money was no object, where would you like to go, what would be your number-one place to travel to?'

'Oh I don't really know,' he said, thinking. 'I quite liked it in Spain.'

Before I met him, I knew, he'd been away quite a lot, often with the fishing family he had lodged with, and he'd always had holidays with parents. But I felt bewildered, even irritated, that of all the wonderful places on the planet, Colin's idea of the trip of a lifetime was Spain, where he'd already been a hundred times.

'Spain?' I repeated incredulously. 'Bloody Spain? Wouldn't you like to go somewhere a bit more interesting, like Japan or Australia?'

'I liked Spain,' he said quietly, but unabashed. 'You asked me where I'd like to go, and that's where I'd like to go. If you don't really want to know where I'd like to go, don't ask me the question.'

I apologised. And when I thought about it afterwards, it reinforced for me the sense that this was a man content with his lot. Unlike me, Colin wasn't dreaming about winning the lottery, or getting away from his day-to-day existence. Why would he? Only fruit flies live in the moment, I used to think – but now I was starting to understand the value of living this way.

And while I did sometimes wish he would strive a bit – because that's how I think people move forward – I was the product of my environment, and so was he. Part of my background was the understanding that we progress, and we have ambitions, and we want to move from one house to another. Colin, however, was someone who was totally unaffected by worldly dreams of success and ambitions. If he had food in the cupboard and the bills were paid and he got a chance to go to Spain, he was happy.

But, really, any bust-ups were rare. All the time, what was drawing me to him was his open heart. Like me, Colin was a Christian – although I wondered at first if he might have said that for my benefit, as he knew how important my faith was to me! But I was relaxed about it: my philosophy is that everyone's on their own journey. And I would say that he was closer to God, in lots of ways, than many people. If it doesn't sound too odd, to me it was in the same way an animal might be, because they are truly being their authentic self, without any agenda.

And Colin's authentic self was a very kind person. He'd always give someone the benefit of the doubt. I, to be honest, was the fiery one.

'I'm bloody annoyed about so-and-so,' I might moan.

Invariably, Colin would say, 'Oh, they're just having a bad day, you've had a bad day before haven't you? Just let it go.'

So he was teaching me to hold things loosely, to choose my battles.

Truly, he was a really kind, generous person who wasn't afraid to be vulnerable – which I feel takes a remarkable degree of self-assurance and confidence. That's real love, when you're prepared to expose who you really are, laying yourself open to judgement or even rejection.

Summer of Love

Our life together began to take shape. If our first date was at sea, afterwards everything we did was based around family. Often we'd go cycling, especially in the evenings, when we'd head down to the seafront and all have an ice cream. When Josh and Henry were at school, if Colin wasn't working – because the weather was too bad for him to be out at sea – we used to go out together during the day. We'd go to nearby Paglesham, where lots of boats are moored, to look at all the yachts and dinghies. You'd think Colin would have had enough of all that, but no! And if he had errands to run for work, things to buy for his trawler, I'd go and get them with him. It might sound boring – but I'd have gone anywhere with him.

We took things quite slowly. 'People always talk about women giving themselves away too soon,' he said. 'But for some of us, it's the same with men. And why should I give myself away to somebody if I don't know if they love me and I can trust them?'

It was eye-opening for me.

'I've never heard a man say that before,' I told him. 'It's very unusual to hear that.'

'Well, why should I feel like I should do something just because all the other f—s do it?'

That's how he spoke, you see – all the fishermen did, it's just the lingo. There's a reason people talk about swearing like a sailor! 'F—ing haul way now! Get those f—s in!' Even Colin's dad used to swear when he was on the boats – though never in front of Colin's mum, and never in front of me. It didn't bother me at all, there was no aggression to it. And Colin was careful never do it in front of the kids – he was quite old-fashioned that way.

Anyway, we didn't wait for ever. One evening, I went to the pub with a couple of girlfriends. We were more than a few drinks in when the conversation came round to men.

'So, Jane – what about you? Have you got your eye on anyone?'

'Oh, I've met this guy,' I told them, stumbling over my words a little. 'He's really gorgeous. Colin, he's a fisherman, he's lovely.'

I admit it, I was completely pissed – so what happened next seemed like a completely sensible idea. 'I know, I'll phone him up,' I said. 'I'll phone him up and you can meet him.'

It wasn't like me to do that, so I must have really wanted to. Well, my friends thought that was a great idea too. 'Oh yeah, ring him, Jane, tell him to come and meet us!'

I had his number in my mobile so dialled it there and then. After a couple of rings, he picked up. 'Hello?' came his voice, croaky with sleep.

'Colin, I'm in Leigh-on-Sea and I'd *love* to see you! Will you come over and meet me?'

There was a pause. 'Ah, bloody hell, give me ten minutes and I'll come and get you. You sound like you're in a right state.'

'Great, I'll see you in a minute!' – and told him where he could pick me up, very pleased with how events were turning out.

Ten minutes later, Colin's battered old car pulled up outside the kebab shop where we were waiting.

'Hello!' I called, waving cheerily – and peered in through the window. Colin, even I could see in my tipsy condition, was not quite dressed for a night out. Because he was wearing pyjama bottoms. Oh, and his woolly hat. When I called he'd been in bed, and had just rolled out from under the covers, pulled on his hat to keep warm, and got in his car.

'Come on,' he said to us, 'I'll give you all a lift home.'

Everyone piled into the back – 'Pleased to meet you, Colin, how are you?' – and I took the front seat next to him.

'Everyone, this is Colin, the man I'm going to marry!' I chorused. 'Isn't that right, Colin?'

'If you say so, darlin', yeah' – unruffled as ever.

Laughing and chatting, we all went back to my little fisherman's cottage and shared a bottle of wine, Colin too. Finally, as my friends disappeared to bunk in my double bed upstairs, Colin and I agreed he'd stay over also.

'You can't drive back to your lodgings now you've had a drink, and we certainly can't wake up Ken next door at this hour,' I pointed out. What no one needed to say was that neither of us wanted him to go. 'I'll just make up the settee for you,' I said, fetching sheets and a duvet.

'Oh all right, thanks darlin'.'

I bustled around him, making the bed. Now it was just the two of us, the house quiet. And of course the inevitable happened, as we both knew it would – I shared the sofa bed with him.

It was just lovely. Colin hadn't had many girlfriends before me, but nothing fazed him. And he seriously surprised me! I just saw again the different sides to him: this easy-going man was also extremely masculine and in control. It was a heady combination, and I felt very safe with him. Really, as a Christian, I should have waited till we were man and wife. But since that first day on his boat, I was totally sure I would marry him; once I knew that, I felt it was okay. And it seemed completely right that, a few months after our first night together, I gave him a front-door key. Not to live with us – we didn't move that fast – but because, under cover of the night, we'd fallen into the habit of him popping in to see me on his way to work.

Being a fisherman meant that the sea dictated when Colin slept and worked, keeping him on a timetable that didn't quite apply to the rest of the world. He would have to go to work whenever the tides were right – and they don't run to a normal working day. If he got up at 1 a.m. one day, it would be around 2 the next day, then 3, 4, 5: a week of earlies, then of lates. I didn't want to go downstairs and open the door at one o'clock in the morning, so it just made sense for him to let himself in. But it was very romantic: to be close, intimate, and so in love, then he'd go off to sea. I'd start the morning with a real smile on my face.

To be frank, we spent a lot of our time together in bed, in those first few months. We were in bed when he first told me how he felt: 'I love you, Jane.'

My heart swelled. I knew that I was in love with him too – and I'd felt that way for a long time. But I didn't say it that night: I wanted him to know that I meant it and wasn't just saying it in response. And I did tell him those precious three words soon after that.

Another night, we were cosy in bed and it was late – three, four o'clock in the morning – and we could hear a car engine sputtering outside. 'Oh, I know what's wrong with that,' said Colin, getting up to help this stranger outside in the small hours. That was just what he was: kind.

Often, the tides would mean he'd leave me sleeping. But if he was in sync with the rest of the world, before he'd set off for work I'd see him go into the back garden. He'd stand and watch the trees, spending a good five minutes working out which way the wind was going and what it might be like later on. Watching from the upstairs window, I'd smile at the serious expression on his face. If the wind was up, you see, the fishermen couldn't go out. If it's windy on land, it's ten times windier on the sea. No fisherman will go out when it's windy – not unless you've got a massive great boat. So a little trawler like Colin's? No. I knew what he was doing, and teased him about 'feeling his barnacles'. But it didn't cross my mind that these were precautions he had to take against a very real danger, out there on the sea. I just had this utter faith that Colin knew what he was doing – any threat seemed so remote.

If he'd had a good day, he'd come back really buzzing and full of adrenalin and – yes – smelly. He could go out at five o' clock in the morning but he might not get back until 14 or 15 hours later, so it was a long day; but then he'd be quite up if it had gone well, and come back with tons of Dover sole for us. He used to stand outside and skin them, so I could cook them. Dover sole is expensive in the shops, but we took it for granted. I'd never cooked it before I met Colin, but I learnt to bake it in tinfoil with butter, salt and pepper and a little white wine; the fish had such a beautiful flavour it never needed too much. So we'd have Dover sole a lot, and lobster; skate would come up in the nets sometimes, too. I really took it for granted having fresh seafood all the time. The other day I went to buy Dover sole in the shops and it was more expensive than steak – I could barely believe it.

Cooking, I soon realised, wasn't one of Colin's skills. His mum had been a great cook, and he'd have early morning breakfasts at cafés or, if he fancied, he could do himself a fry-up and bacon sandwiches. But he wasn't a big eater – he'd go days without eating sometimes, and then he'd have days when he wouldn't stop eating. But he never ate when he wasn't hungry and he wouldn't dream of eating just because it was a mealtime: perhaps because he was used to living and working to a different rhythm to everyone on land. He must have been doing something right, though, because he was very slim, and muscly.

The first time we went shopping together was a revelation. Colin was still lodging in Thorpe Bay, which is just a few miles from Leigh, with the fishing family he had worked for as a very young man. That was a long-standing arrangement: when he'd started out working for them, he would cycle over – he was only 16, so he didn't drive – and sometimes had to be there at one o'clock in the morning. So, when he had early starts like that, it made sense that he'd stay the night. The reality was, however, that by that time he was spending much of his free time at my house. 'I eat at yours all the time, I'll pay for the shopping,' he told me, so off we went to Asda. But when I picked up a basket, as I always did, he stopped me.

'A basket? What are you doing? Get a trolley.'

'Well, I never get a trolley's worth,' I explained.

'Oh, just go and get a trolley and stop arguing for once in your life, darlin'.'

So I did.

But then, as we were walking along the aisle, I watched him throwing in crisps, biscuits, all sorts.

'No, you've got to put them back, we don't need those,' I said.

'I know we don't need those,' said Colin, 'but I work bloody hard all week and I like them!'

It was a revelation, strange as that sounds. I thought, God, is this what people do? They go shopping and they don't just buy what they need. They buy pots of cream!

They buy olives! They buy things they *like*, not just what they need.

Looking back, I suspect Colin was displaying his peacock feathers a little, because I wouldn't spend that much even now, when things are a bit easier financially compared to when I met him. Perhaps he was just trying to impress me, though. It wasn't bravado, so much as that he wanted to please me and the boys; not, 'Look how much Golden Wonder I can buy,' so much as, 'Let me do this for you. I know that you don't have this, so let me treat you all.'

In fact, pretty much all the things he got were for the children. Colin had a sweet tooth so he bought chocolates and lovely things for the kids – and him! – and other nice food: olives, sundried tomatoes, all this stuff that I might get at Christmas, as a real treat. And he liked steak, too, I remember. We never had steak!

When we went to pay for it, it came to £130. Now, I had never in my life spent £130 on shopping, ever. So when it totalled that much I was mortified.

I said to him at the till, 'Do you want me to put something back?'

'Of course not,' he said. 'Why?'

'Because it's £130.'

And it wasn't an issue.

It became an issue, later on, when the fishing got scarcer and the weather was bad. When it meant that he couldn't work for weeks and weeks we did have to adopt my frugal cooking again. But when our financial situation was all right – which it often was, in the summer – he used to treat us to things. He wasn't extravagant, he didn't buy bottles of champagne, he didn't buy steak every week. In fact, it was what I now know many households do. But, at that time, I had just been existing in a different world.

Before I met Colin, you see, my excursions with the children were totally limited to where I could get to on the bus – and afford. I used to take them to free attractions, museums and so on in school holidays, but it would be one or two trips a year because money was so tight. I had loads of friends who were single parents too, and most of them were completely broke as well. We'd make a picnic, go to the park, go to the beach – take a bottle of wine between us. We couldn't buy fish and chips and seafood, things like that. It just didn't happen.

So, having a man with a car was like a whole world opening to us. I'd never had a car in my adult life, but Colin always did – loads of them in the time I knew him! They were always old bangers. The Land Rover was his favourite and that was the car that was most him: oily, diesel, a bloke's car, in military green. One of his fishing friends had sold it to him for a pound.

'Let's jump in the car – we'll go to Clacton for the day,' he'd say. Which doesn't sound like a lot of fun, but when it's someone that you're mad about, he could say, 'Let's take a walk through a pile of manure' and you'd think it was the best invitation ever – at least, at that time I probably would have thought so! I'd have followed him anywhere.

Another day, he took us all to Maldon Park for the first

time, a local beauty spot that I'd never visited even though it was a 45-minute drive away. We had a wonderful day at this beautiful park on the banks of the River Blackwater, with an adventure playground and loads of things for the children. It may sound trivial, but it wasn't. I felt normal again – because I'd known that other people did this sort of thing, but we didn't. I just felt as if he was bringing so much to our family. I didn't realise how outside of normal I had been existing. I had been inhabiting this strange periphery – and I hadn't even been aware of it.

It was a very special time, those gentle summer days, just me and Colin in our own little world, getting to know more and more about each other.

Blending Two Lives

It was one balmy summer evening when, with my house full of women, Colin turned up at my door, unplanned.

Because funds were always so limited, I didn't go out very much, but I used to have, every week, a girls' night. There was a core group – my good friend Angee, a nurse and a true eccentric, was a stalwart – and they'd often bring their friends too, so sometimes there would be five of us, sometimes 25. And we didn't just lounge about and talk. We'd play word games, like the Radio 4 game *Just a Minute*, get our guitars out, sing. None of us were the sort of women who enjoyed sitting around saying, 'Do you know where so-and-so's going on holiday,' or 'Where did you get your dress?' – it would have reduced us to comas. It was very much a fun night, a creative, stimulating evening. We did talk, of course, and I had told them all I'd met someone, but I downplayed it. I wasn't ready to start shouting everything from the rooftops – this was too new, too fragile, too special to be held up to scrutiny yet.

Some people love visitors coming unannounced; I hate it. It's because I've got a bit of Rain Man syndrome: my friends always say of me, 'Bloody Jane, you've got to make an appointment to see her,' but it's just because I have to work myself up to it. I love company, but I really enjoy my own space too, and I do prefer to know when someone's coming, so I can mentally prepare for it. I could spend endless amounts of time on my own and not be lonely. Perhaps that was something I had in common with Colin. So, him turning up unannounced when I had guests threw me a bit.

Then I took in the view – and it threw me a lot more! Now, I am not fashion-conscious at all. But Colin, re-member, used to play Chas and Dave in his car and was as close as you could get to someone who had just been plonked on this planet. As I've said, he had none of the same terms of reference as many of us. If I asked him, 'Do you remember watching *Steptoe*?' – referring to the old sitcom – he'd say, blankly, 'No.' He had never really watched TV in his life, because his whole existence was about nature and the sea. He enjoyed *Only Fools and Horses* and we both loved *The Vicar of Dibley*. Later, we'd watch it with the boys, all roaring with laughter.

Yes, he might have listened to Radio 1, he might have watched the news, might have read a paper that had been left around the fish shop, but he did not seek out informa-tion from the outside world. It wasn't because he was a stupid man – it was because he had a very big internal life, and he was satisfied. I found him fascinating, partly because he'd built a life around who he was and how he genuinely responded to things – I really liked that. The flipside to all this freedom from media indoctrination, however, was that he was also almost entirely free from any sort of influence as to what 'normal' people wore!

So, Colin that night was wearing these jaw-droppingly grim, geeky shoes – really old-fashioned, shiny black loafer things – old jeans, and, the crowning glory, a Christmas jumper. Oh, and it was summer. Colin would simply have put that jumper on because he was chilly, he wouldn't have given a second thought to the design of it; it was purely functional. I learnt to love that and appreciate it – after a while! I really did. But when it's the early days and you've got your friends round and you've been telling them about this man you've met and bigging him up a bit, and he turns up fresh off the boat – quite literally – in any old get-up . . . let's just say, I could have done without the Christmas jumper! What should I do? I was really torn, because I was falling for him, but I wasn't sure if I was ready to see if my friends saw how special he was, too. So I decided not to chance it, not just yet.

'Oh excuse me a moment,' I called to everyone in the living room, as I briskly ushered Colin into the kitchen.

'Look,' I planned to tell him, 'I've got my girlfriends round now, I only see them once a week, can we get together later?' And then usher him back out, everyone none the wiser.

Well, that was the plan – but my friends weren't going to let a chance like this go by. They swarmed into the kitchen, instantly sizing up the situation and falling over each other to say hello. 'Oh, are you Colin, really nice to meet you, oh we've heard so much about you!' There was never going to be any stopping you lot from finding out what was going on, I thought to myself. Of course, he won them all over. He was funny and charming and it was absolutely fine – in fact, he spent the whole evening with us. I'd been worried about nothing.

By that point I'd been on my own for ages, so my friends were so happy for me that I'd met Colin, but they were fascinated by him, as his own person, as well. That night, they all wanted to know the same things everybody always did: what do you catch, when did you start being a fisherman, how did you get into it, can anybody be a fisherman? In a world where everything's so sanitised, wrapped in cellophane and plastic, it's a very manly job – and Colin was a very masculine man, and I think women liked that. At least, this one did!

After that, he was one of our gang, coming to the gigs we went to and becoming part of my world. 'How's Pugwash?' they used to ask me. On paper, I knew, they couldn't have been more different: all my friends were musicians or members of the church I went to, in Southend, which had quite a bohemian congregation. But my fisherman just became part of that. We used to go and see our friends play in bands and a group of us would nearly always end up back at our house around the table with a bottle of wine, guitars out.

Colin, however, wasn't used to drinking very much, as he wasn't a massive socialiser. Part of that was because his hours could be unsociable. In fact, if we were invited somewhere, I'd always have to check the tide timetables to see if he'd be out fishing or not, and I often went out on my own if he needed to get to bed for a very early start.

One night, the consequences of our two worlds colliding were suddenly brought home to me. We'd gone out to a wine bar in Leigh – neither of us were really the wine bar type, but that's where our friends had gathered – and, as the night went on, Colin, I noticed, had been quietly clocking up the brandy and Cokes. No matter, I thought, he worked very hard, so if he fancied a few drinks who'd blame him? It was not as if anyone would notice either; he was hardly rowdy by nature. And that was the moment he decided to start taking his shirt off.

'What the hell are you doing?' I hissed at him, as all our crowd started falling about laughing.

'I'm expressing myself!' he kept saying. 'I'm expressing myself!'

For some reason, the drink had completely gone to his head that night. Thankfully, he didn't get much beyond the shirt – and I did see the funny side. The thing was, he was so quiet, it was just a complete personality change. Our friends used to tease him about it for ages afterwards: 'You going to start expressing yourself tonight, Colin?'

Our families met each other, too. I really liked his sister Wendy, mother to two boys, who I thought was like a female version of Colin – hard-working, cuddly, warm, loving, with the same dark hair – in fact the whole family were like that. My parents loved him: he did loads of jobs for them, repaired their fence and so on. It was very easy to rely on him. He was never scratchy or irritable; just really good-natured.

Mum'd ring up: 'Oh, Colin, we've got a problem with one of our pipes.'

'Don't you worry about that, darlin', I'll pop in on my way home from work.' And he'd have a cup of tea, make them feel like the centre of the universe. I really liked that about him.

Much of the time, though, it would just be me, Colin – my 'Cobbs' – and the boys, which I loved. We used to go on the sea with him quite a lot, although it was tricky because he'd have to lose a whole day's earnings to take us out. As a child, he used to go out with his dad when he was working, but it just wouldn't have appealed to my little landlubbers: they'd have got bored. Still, when we could, we used to go out on his skiff, the smaller boat he used to reach his trawler, *Louisa*, and head out to the Maplin Sands, a huge stretch of mudflats off the Essex coast.

We'd find a sandbank that you can only access when the tide's out. It's really strange sand, very soft, with no pebbles, so you almost feel like you're abroad – and even the waves come in differently, rolling in with big gaps between them. You can still see the shore, but you're probably a quarter of a mile out. Because you can only get there by boat, there'd be nobody else there, and it would feel like we were on a desert island, just the four of us. We'd have a picnic on the empty sands, play frisbee and once the water started rising we'd climb back into the skiff and set off again.

Something else we loved to do was take the boys down to Leigh's old town, along the seafront, where you've got all the little cockle sheds and the big seafood restaurants, cafés and pubs. And there's a fishermen's co-operative as well, selling the local catch. People come from all over to buy cockles especially – it's a rich area for the shellfish, with millions growing on the cockle beds in the estuary. They don't look particularly nice when you open up the shells – they're orange and grey inside – but they taste of the sea. I got into shellfish in my teens, when I discovered it for myself. My parents didn't buy it, but I loved it. So, Colin and I would have a pint and we'd all share a pot or two of prawns, just out of a little polystyrene tub. Or, if there were a few of us out for a drink, we might order a seafood platter: you get local cockles, mussels, whelks, all the little shellfish that are sold, crab too. You'd get a wine bottle filled with vinegar – dark brown vinegar – and white pepper to season it. People do buy prawn cocktail sauce, but that's not really what it's eaten with, not if you're a local anyway; it's eaten with white pepper and vinegar.

Another thing that all the locals know about is that in Old Leigh we've a little beach – secret, almost. Tourists, you see, will always head to Southend if they want sand, and really it's only locals who know Leigh's a beach too, right next to the Smack pub, with lots of little cafés selling ice creams, and bucket-and-spade shops. I'd been going there since my teens and Colin and I spent a lot of time down there with the boys – it was free, and healthy! We'd make a picnic, take the short cut through the little park at the top, Library Gardens, and down the steps onto the beach, where we'd eat sandwiches that would always end up full of sand – but tasty, all the same.

Sometimes, Colin would take the boys out on his own too – to the park, to play football – while I sorted stuff at home. In fact, he was fantastic with the boys, so patient – often a lot more patient than me. Because I'd been a single parent for so long, I had never really understood what it meant to have a really good father figure around all the time. I always used to say that a single parent can do just as good a job as anyone – and they can, absolutely – but when you've a partner by your side you see the difference. You've got the practical help of another adult whose views you trust, balancing, supporting and challenging your own decisions on parenting day in, day out.

Then there's a deep understanding that comes from being the same gender as somebody else. My two boys had always got on really well, but as they developed into adolescence they would argue sometimes – more and more, it often felt. It didn't help that where we lived was very small and they shared a tiny room. One day, their argument got so heated it was on the verge of becoming physical, which really upset me. Colin calmed the situation down and told me, 'Look, they're just like two young stags getting territorial; you mustn't worry about it,' giving me a hug. 'It's the equivalent of pissing on a bush! Don't worry, I'll take one of them out, give them a bit of space.' He was so reassuring and provided an insight into male behaviour that I just didn't have.

It helped, too, that he was interested in (or at least pretended to be) the same things that they were – computer games, wrestling – and he'd join in. I liked music and museums, and the boys did too, but they were young boys growing into young men and that insight he had was really valuable. And, while I had to go through the motions, he enjoyed it. For a time, they were really into the World Wresting Federation – those pumped-up men in shiny leotards throwing each other about a ring – and would copy the moves they saw on TV. 'Stop doing that,' was my automatic reaction. 'You're going to knock something over!' Colin, on the other hand, would put all the cushions on the floor, say, 'Come on,' and have a knockabout with them. It was like animals in the wild, playing, and it helped bind us all together as a family.

But he wasn't all macho with them, far from it. One day, we were watching TV together when an old Bruce Lee film – so full of martial arts, and flashy fighting stunts, but very tame by today's standards – came on.

Colin turned to me. 'You've got to turn that off, darlin',' he said. 'It's completely unsuitable for these boys.'

'Why?' I said. 'It's only a Bruce Lee film.'

And of course the boys joined in too, keener than ever to watch it after hearing that they shouldn't. 'Why? Why can't we watch it, Mum?'

'It's much too violent,' said Colin, quiet but firm. 'I don't think they should see it.'

I paused, but I couldn't really see a problem: Josh and

Henry were 13 and 11 by this point, old enough for some PG-rated old flick.

'Look, Colin, it's not an 18, I'm sure they can cope.'

'No, really,' said Colin. 'It's got one of the most horrific scenes that I've ever witnessed.'

So I let the boys watch the film only on the condition that when Colin told them to look away, they would. 'Do you promise?'

'We promise,' they swore, very solemn.

So the moment came – this scene that was apparently the most horrific one Colin had seen – and the boys dutifully looked away. And the scene was so tame I couldn't believe it! The thing was, Colin hated violence, he couldn't bring himself to watch anything violent on TV. So he was being very protective of the boys in this instance, even though he didn't really need to.

It was very sweet.

We did tease him afterwards, though. When we got our kitten, Guinness, it would be: 'Oh careful, don't let Colin near it. It's probably one of the most horrific things he's ever seen!' And if the kitten would play with a ball of wool, or a feather, the boys and I would be joking: 'Careful, it's so violent!'

'You horrible lot!' he'd say, and laugh. 'I was only trying to be caring!'

Because he really was caring. Another time, the fair came into town. We were all enjoying ourselves, eating candyfloss and playing on the stalls, when one of the bigger attractions, a terrifying-looking thing that whirled you about all over the place, caught Colin's eye.

'Come on,' he said to the boys. 'Let's go on.' They weren't keen on those sorts of rides. 'It's not scary,' said Colin. 'Let's do it!'

'No, really,' said Josh. 'We're just not into it – we'll go on the dodgems, but we don't really want to go on this ride.'

I chimed in. 'Look, they don't like them, Colin. They don't want to.'

Of course, he wouldn't force them – but he did try to encourage them another way.

'I'll get on,' he said, adding under his breath: 'If they can see me do it, and I'm all right, then maybe they'll go on again with me.'

And off he went, strapped into a little car. And it went so fast, whirled around upside down, side to side, all over the place, that the three of us on the ground felt completely justified in staying put. After what seemed like ages, the ride finally came to an end.

Poor Colin wobbled off completely green. 'I think you were right to stay off it, boys!'

We felt so sorry for him, because we knew he would have hated it – but it was funny.

Learning the Ropes

At the same time as I was learning more about Colin, I was learning more about this world of his. Despite growing up in a seaside town, I'd been totally oblivious to the community under my nose. It's understandable, looking back: I was into Pink Floyd, Crosby, Stills, Nash and Young and playing spin-the-bottle in the park as a teenager – that's what kept me busy.

My family had no link to the fishing community, either. My parents were Londoners, born and bred. They met at the Ministry of Education, where they both worked, and moved to Leigh to start a family. But in the end Mum and Dad tried for years and years to have a baby, and fostered, before they eventually adopted a baby: me. Then, as so often happens, within three years of that Mum had fallen pregnant with my brother, Robin. My parents never knew why they had struggled to have children, and it was always my suspicion that when you're in that sort of stress mode your body just knows you're not in a good place to have a child. So many of us adopted people have siblings who are their parents' biological children: it's almost as if, once the pressure's off, your body thinks, I can relax now!

Dad stayed a civil servant. He had trained as a graphic

artist – before the days of computer fonts, he'd do lettering, calligraphy, cartoons – but the war changed everything. He ended up in the Southend office of the Inland Revenue, but I think he remained an artist at heart. He's very political – left-wing – and very smart and gregarious. Robin, my brother, and I absorbed a lot from him about how to be with people. Mum worked from home as a dressmaker, using a huge knitting machine that she'd taught herself how to use. I remember her sitting over it, cigarette in mouth – everybody seemed to smoke back then. But she had been evacuated at four years old and I believe it had cast a shadow over the rest of her life. Some kids, maybe, can shrug off being sent away with a label round their neck and a gas mask – 'It's an adventure' – but she'd been a shy little girl. As an adult, she was creative, kind and sweet, but she found the world quite frightening and preferred the sanctuary of her home.

That meant our family life involved a lot of indoor activities: card games, darts, table football, board games; I never really went to the beach much as a kid, even though I love swimming, love the water. I made my own fun. Mum had been a shorthand typist in London, so I'd inherited her beautiful old Imperial typewriter. By the time I was six or seven, I could type and change the ribbons, and spent huge amounts of time writing stories and turning them into 'library' books, with my poor brother facing daily visits to the library (my bedroom) to make his selection. Once, when I was 10, I organised a carnival with the children from the roads around ours. I told them to dress up, and all we did was walk round the streets, but one of the kids' mums rang the local paper. That was the first time I made the press. Perhaps that gave me a taste for it! I staged a play too, in the local scout hut – all the parents had to sit with their backs to us for a quarter of an hour while we had our first rehearsal – and another time I held an 'Olympics'. So I didn't miss what I didn't know: my world was the streets I grew up in.

But it did explain, perhaps, why Colin was the first fisherman I'd ever met. There were quite a few surprises. I had not expected it to be such a solitary job. I knew that there were not many fishermen left in Leigh-on-Sea: perhaps half a dozen working out of the village at that time; the same again in nearby Southend. And then there were the cockle men, who outnumbered the fishermen – perhaps eight or so working from Leigh's old town. Still, I suppose if I thought about it all, I expected that the fishermen would do a day's work, then retire to the pub afterwards, all 'Ooh arr, didn't we have a good day of fish' over a pint each.

That wasn't really the case. Even if Colin had been a pub person, the stocks are scarce and it's competitive. The reality is that there's not enough fish to go round, people are not always earning enough to survive, and that does not make for a particularly celebratory environment. Some days Colin would catch stones of fish – and some days nothing.

So, if he did find a good spot at sea with a lot of fish and wanted to go back the next day, he'd try and make sure no one followed him – and all the time he'd be trying to keep an eye on what other people were doing, too. A fisherman,

I also learnt, might not always be quite honest about the size of his catches to his rivals. One of them might say, 'Oh, I caught 30 stone today,' and Colin would tell me later, 'Thirty stone my arse, there was nothing there, I went there yesterday.' Everybody was trying to keep up 'face', as he used to call it.

That said, as much as the competition was real, underpinning it all was this understanding that they were, at heart, in it together. Just the other day I found a newspaper cutting that reminded me of a time when they'd rallied round. Once, when Colin needed help with some repairs on his boat that were going to prove very expensive, a flotilla of fishermen came from miles around to help him out. It made the local paper, but I knew he would have done the same for any of them without a second thought.

You see, his dad Ken would have fished with their dads and grandads too, in many cases – the ties went way back. Once Ken explained to me just how far. I'd got to know Ken then, through Colin, and it was a case of like father, like son: Ken was a warm, gentle, soft-spoken man. He and his wife hadn't really been drinkers, but they'd come back from their summer holidays in Spain or Portugal with a bottle of something, so I'd go round and be offered some sort of exotic liqueur no one had ever touched: 'Have a drink, have a drink.' I'd be sipping this massively alcoholic prune juice, or something similar, and Ken would talk to me.

'In the 1800s, my forefathers fished exactly the same grounds as Colin does now,' he told me, with quiet pride.

Ken's grandfather, Arthur Dolby, had a boat called the *Mabel Evelyn*, while Ken's father – also Arthur, but known as 'Wonkeye' – had the *Britannia*; his brother John would fish from the *Girl Heather*. Ken didn't know why his dad had been called Wonkeye, but most fishermen had nicknames. His uncle, also Arthur, had been 'Goldking' as he'd always boast about his earnings, while he remembered one chap nicknamed Nunner, because when he hauled his nets up he'd say, 'Look, I got anunner one!' Colin's got off quite lightly with me just calling him Cobbs, I thought.

Speaking to his dad, I'd feel such a sense of history: Ken's father had started off fishing from a sailboat, and had only started using an engine in 1934. Ken had gone to work full-time with his dad at 14 years old. It was expected of him that he'd go to sea, the profession handed down father to son, just as it would be with him and Colin.

'As a boy he'd go running from school right down to Old Leigh when the boat was coming in, to meet me and help me lift the fish off,' he remembered.

'That's really young!' I'd say. 'My parents wouldn't even let me go to the park on my own.'

But they just lived a different sort of life – Colin had had a lot of freedom. He didn't go to school very much, he really just wanted to be out on the boat with his dad.

And there was such a treasure chest of knowledge passed down through the generations. Today, fishermen would likely struggle to do a day's work without their navigational aids and electronic fishing devices. (Wrecks, I learnt, remain a big problem, and can do thousands of pounds worth of damage to your nets, or boat.) But all that information used to be handed down via charts, or just from father to son, as it had been from Ken's dad to him, and from him to Colin. In fact, Ken told me, Colin had only recently joined the age of technology after working with the old-fashioned charts for years. That didn't really surprise me! After all, I knew he'd barely used a cashpoint.

But Ken had seen a lot of change. Shrimping had stopped being a liveable trade by the 1970s, he told me, as the creeks which fed the Thames filled with chemicals from domestic and industrial waste, killing off the tiny animals the shrimp needed to feed on. The way people shopped altered, too. When he'd been young, he used to go round people's houses selling shrimps, but people didn't want them any more, he said, couldn't be bothered fiddling around and peeling them – they wanted the prepared, frozen stuff.

The fish stocks, meanwhile, had got lower and lower. That was why, I learnt, there were very strict rules, across the European Union, about how much the fishermen were allowed to catch – how much of each species, and what size fish – in an attempt to protect the declining stocks from overfishing. But what this could mean in practice was that Colin, if he was lucky enough to have a good day, would have to throw fish back into the water as he reached his quota limits. After all, it wasn't as if you could just fish for the one type and ask the rest to stay out of your nets. (Although, having said that, perhaps that *was* almost the idea – the rules were very strict about nets, and whether the mesh was too big or too small, as that would affect what species and age of fish you caught.)

The sickening thing was, Colin told me, that the fish you threw back were usually dead already. The flatfish, in particular, even if they had survived, would sometimes just float on the surface, unable to get back to the bottom of the sea again. I thought it was a crazy waste. You'd catch these fish, they'd die, being out of the water, and then you'd have to throw them back. And they really did keep tabs: the fisheries people did spot checks, so they could come in on a helicopter or a boat, or could be waiting on the causeway when you unloaded. There's been a lot of pressure since then to get the system changed and I'm glad. Colin found it heartbreaking – all the fishermen did. In fact, in 2007 Colin and some of the other local fishermen actually sailed down the Thames to Parliament, forming an 'armada' of fishing boats, to protest against the quota system.

And don't think that you could just buy a boat and set out to make your fortune – oh no. You've got to have a fishing vessel licence and they are expensive and not always easy to get. You can't obtain one without safety at sea training and various other things, but without one you can't operate a boat.

Still, they weren't as hard to come by as the cockle licences. Colin once did a season as crew on one of the cockle boats, which use a suction technique to suck up the shellfish from the seabed. Yes, he had his own boat, but that didn't offer a guaranteed income – he could go out and not catch anything. So, for about three months he took a job for a fixed wage doing three or four days a week and the rest of the time he went fishing on the *Louisa*. He loved it – I think he would have liked to have kept doing it, because of the money.

Colin spoke well of one local cockle man in particular: Michael Bates. 'Prince Michael of Sealand, he's a real gent,' he'd said one day, totally matter-of-fact.

'Prince who of what?' I'd asked, raising an eyebrow.

I'd stumbled into a strange piece of British history. Sealand, Colin explained, was a tower in the North Sea, built by the government as a fortress to protect us during the Second World War. Michael's late father, Roy, had claimed it as his own after the war and – stay with me – declared it a principality, complete with its own currency, stamps and king: Roy! He'd faced off the British government, an attempted invasion, even a coup. He was like Essex's very own James Bond, I thought.

'So there's royalty among the Leigh fishermen.' I laughed.

Anyway, it was hard for Colin to get into cockling permanently. The set-up was a bit like season tickets for football, I thought: though the cockle licences could potentially sell on for a fortune, sales were rare and more often than not they were passed down through families.

The cocklers also had quite a good system to manage the stocks of the shellfish, Colin said. There was a strict season, which meant they were not allowed to start cockling – harvesting the shellfish – before a certain date, and they had to finish on a certain date. It was an arrangement which allowed the cockles to breed so that the stocks were replenished.

In contrast, after a lean winter, the fishermen would be desperate to go back on the river to start work again. But as the fish came in from the North Sea to breed in the Thames, as the Dover sole do, if they went out too early nearly everything they caught would be pregnant, laden with roe – which, of course, affected the breeding cycle and the future stocks.

Thinking about the future, sometimes I couldn't help but feel a little sad. Colin had been just four years old on his first day's fishing with Ken; his mum Joyce, brother Ian and sister Wendy all used to go too – it was quite the family event. But Ken couldn't see how the family business would continue (his other son, Ian, was nautical, but he'd gone into the Merchant Navy rather than fishing), what with the pressures on the fish stocks and the other ways the world was changing.

I learnt, too, about the risks involved. Many people don't know this, but working as a fisherman is classed as the most dangerous peacetime job there is. It's not just the physical side of it, though that's incredibly tough; it's the emotional demands of it too – out there, on the waves, you're very far from the day-to-day world back on land. Don't think that because Colin fished on the Thames, this was some gentle jaunt on the waves. He'd go right to the edges of the Thames Estuary, where the river water meets salt – the North Sea. Out there, all you can see is water. His dad Ken had sometimes acted as his mate – an extra pair of hands on board – but he was getting too old, really, to do it when I knew Colin. It's quite a climb getting from a skiff to a trawler, out on the waves. And Colin would not have hired anyone, the reason being simply that he never earned enough to do so. So he was out there on his own, for hours and hours on end.

Still, Colin certainly didn't spend time fretting about what could happen out at sea. He would tell me, 'Oh, it's really dangerous,' but in the same way, I thought, that you might say, 'Oh, driving your car's really dangerous' – you don't think anything's going to happen to you. It's not unless you've seen a car crash, or someone you know has been involved in one, that you feel the effects. I knew, intellectually, that if you're on a boat and it goes over, you could drown. But I made no emotional connection. I couldn't imagine it – Colin was so sure and certain, so experienced and confident. He wasn't a good swimmer, no, but a lot of the fishermen aren't. Maybe it's because they've spent so much time on the water, they've never bothered going in it. As he said, even if you could swim, it wouldn't save you if something went wrong far out at sea. Likewise, he didn't normally wear a life jacket, just as a lot of them don't. Colin was just brought up in a world that had little overlap with the modern health and safety culture, and taking precautions against every eventuality.

That may sound strange, I know. It's tradition – they never have worn a life jacket – and if they've survived this long, why should they start now? They say it affects their mobility, that they can't move about how they need to on the boat. And it's true, in the past apparently there hasn't really been a good life jacket that has been easy and practical to wear and won't get in the way for fishermen. (I'm told there's now a new style, designed by fishermen for fishermen, so perhaps that's no longer the case.)

But above all else, I suspect, it's the belief that it's never going to happen to them. 'I'm not going to be the one that ends up in the sink,' as they call it. 'It's never going to happen to me.' And if you're wearing a life jacket, in a way you are acknowledging what could happen to you, what dangers you face daily. That's a difficult thing to do.

Of course, none of that occupied my thoughts in those more innocent days. And Colin was not one to worry about what hadn't happened. I don't think it crossed his mind that a situation could arise that he might not be able to handle. He'd been out there on his dad's boat, his grandad's boat, his great-grandad's boat, in good weather and in bad.

He'd just say, 'Oh, it was a difficult old time getting home to you', 'I had to work hard to get home tonight darling!' And life went on.

The Wind in My Sails

When I first met Colin, I was occasionally singing with a friend very casually, in a local pub on a Sunday night. It wasn't a proper gig – my stage fright put paid to anything like that. It was an informal affair, sitting round the bar tables amid a crowd of our friends, us all singing together. We were 'paid' in beer and maybe my taxi fare home, but I just liked the opportunity to make music. When that drew to an end, I didn't stop. In the evenings I would play my guitar and write songs for no other reason than why some people might knit, or collect stamps; it was just my hobby. I never played them to anybody but I used to record them using an old cassette player.

Still, even after Colin and I had known each other a few months, I didn't mention the songs I'd record at home. While I was getting to know the fishing world, Colin had yet to learn about the music I loved to create. Because it's a bit like showing someone your poems – you think, I like doing this, but are they, in fact, a bit rubbish? There's a difference, too, between writing something that you feel, singing and recording it for your own ears, and actually sharing it with someone; my songs were never meant for public consumption.

But when I did eventually play some of my songs, stuff I'd written years previously, Colin reacted so positively – his usual encouraging self, I knew by then.

'Oh they're great, they're brilliant, they really are,' he said. 'Why don't you record them properly?'

'Well, I don't really know how to,' I said. 'I don't really know how to go about it. I think it's expensive.'

And I was right. Nonetheless, Colin, bless his heart, encouraged and paid for me to record these songs properly. Love is deaf as well as blind, I thought. But a friend of mine, a producer, had a studio at home and did me a deal. He made a living at it, making recordings for local bands, and was very talented.

Before I knew it, we'd recorded a handful of songs and, these being the days before iTunes, produced a run of CDs: 1,000, the shortest run you could do. I didn't know how to negotiate then; it didn't cross my mind as it would now to say, well, I'll just have 250.

I gave all my friends and family a CD but after that I didn't know what to do with them.

And so I was left with 950 CDs stacked in boxes in my bedroom.

If you're performing, you can sell them at gigs, but I wasn't performing anywhere. Worse, there was still the stage fright. While I'd enjoyed my nights in a duo at the pub, I had no plans to take to a bigger stage. I know, I thought, I'll post this off to Richard Branson and he'll think, oh, Kylie's looking for a song. I soon realised that wasn't how it worked.

And then, Colin mentioned that I had something of a deadline. 'Oh, I've got to start paying that loan back,' he mentioned one day. It turned out that he had taken out one of those loans that gave you three months' grace and then you had to start repaying it. Now, until then, I hadn't known he had had to get a loan to do this – he hadn't told me. Bloody hell, I thought, what am I going to do? I didn't know how on earth I was going to shift these CDs. I had this terrible guilt that Colin had had this faith in me and done this lovely thing for me. It wasn't a fortune that he'd borrowed – £1,500 or something – but of course I wanted to repay him. You know what it's like when you fall in love with somebody, you want to be the best version of yourself. So I had fire in my belly.

Now, around that time I started doing some part-time work from home for an industry music magazine that a friend of mine had set up. Mark and I had been in a band together back in the day in our twenties. We'd have practice nights when we'd have a few beers, play a few songs, but we only made it out of the rehearsal room once. I think we thought someone would walk by and hear us whistling and give us a record deal! We didn't even have a name. Still, while we were all mates and loved making music together, Mark had his head screwed on a bit more than the rest of us and had set up a magazine. I was his editorial assistant, which meant I had to read the press releases that record companies and publicists would send in, change the information to the house style and send them back to him, so they could run in the news pages.

The work meant that I needed to get online for the first time, in order that Mark, as the editor, could email me the press releases. So Colin, bless him, bought us a little computer and got us signed up for the internet. And I was totally hooked. I was born to be online! The community of it, typing a message and sending it to the other side of the world at the press of a button – I just loved it. It still fascinates me now. One day, playing about, I idly typed into a search engine a question. 'How can you sell CDs if you haven't got a record deal?'

Well, the floodgates well and truly opened. I discovered a whole world of unsigned music, a global DIY cottage industry, made up of people like me – passionate about music, but not part of the world of big record companies and charts and deals. It was a total revelation to me that you could bypass all the industry's receptionists and PAs and just do it yourself, the internet making it possible for music makers and fans to find each another without a record company to connect them. And if other people can do it, so can I, I thought.

One company's name in particular kept coming up. It seemed wherever I found an unsigned artist doing well, they were selling their music via CD Baby. I looked up the website. Here were step-by-step instructions for setting up a webpage with music samples to sell your CDs online. There was also an entire section about promotion and how best to get your music heard. So I just followed the instructions, adding my own ideas – and, surprisingly quickly, started getting results. It was such a buzz. Soon

I started writing to other websites that sold CDs asking if they would consider selling unsigned music also. I got my music up there, too, and then I realised I had to get it reviewed, so began tracking down music fans, bloggers, journalists and reviewers who would review unsigned bands. I was really motivated, and thoroughly enjoying this side of the music business.

The bottom line was that I sold lots of CDs – but that said far more about my selling technique than the quality of the music, I thought! Still, if I didn't have heaps of confidence in my songwriting, some people must have liked them and I was thrilled about that. I'd managed to pay Colin back and, purely by chance, I'd found something I was good at: promotion.

And the experience had a broader impact on my life. The local paper ran a story about me, how I'd managed to sell all those CDs, and other bands started getting in touch with me to see if I could help them sell their records too, and so for years – years – I did that for other musicians. Really, it was what I know now to be PR, although back then I never charged a penny. I just knew that I loved getting excited about things. In fact, I would only offer to help people if I was passionate about their work, thinking: if I'm not a genuine fan, how the hell could I convince anyone else to be?

It wasn't until it was taking up more and more of my time that Colin said, 'This is mad, you've got to start charging.' I didn't have the confidence, thinking that when you start charging, you can't make a mistake. Of course, he was right – and I did eventually start charging people, though not over the odds. The very first 'proper' PR job I did was a three-month campaign for somebody, which got them loads of coverage, for £50!

Still, those small beginnings signalled that I'd been set on a new path in life – and for that I had Colin, who'd had faith in me, to thank.

Baby on Board

At the start of the new millennium, Colin and I had quite a surprise. We thought we were being careful, but clearly we weren't that careful, because I missed a period. I waited a couple of weeks – 'It could be stress, maybe I've got the dates wrong,' I told him – but if you've had a child before, as I had, you recognise the symptoms and deep down I knew. I did a test.

Positive.

Standing there in my bathroom, holding the little plastic stick, the biggest shock to me wasn't that I was going to have a baby, it was what it meant. I love Colin and I know that I will marry him, I thought – but this is something that was supposed to happen at some time in the unspecified future! There was no hurry. And yet, nature had decided a different course for us.

My mind started whirling. I was thrilled to be having his baby – this was the man that I was head over heels in love with – but at the same time I felt that everything was being rushed. That made me anxious. After all, we weren't even properly living together yet. Yes, Colin was round all the time – he used to pop in for his tea every night – but still, I quite liked him 'officially' being next door. For me, there was something about having another grown-up in your space and having to compromise. I was the one who was the commitment-phobe, truth be told, so I quite liked him going next door on occasion! It really was the best of both worlds.

But if I stuck to my usual role of being the worrier, Colin – fortunately – was as upbeat and as ready to embrace change as ever. 'I can't wait to tell my dad,' he said, giving me a kiss. He couldn't believe that he was going to be a father; he was just so thrilled. The thing was that, at 38, he thought that all this had passed him by: children, marriage, a family of his own. It was as if what was happening was so unexpected, and he was so glad of it that he welcomed every aspect of the experience. His joy was infectious; as the smile spread over his face that day, I couldn't help but share his excitement.

That night we took the boys to the Three Shells, a little café on the seafront, and told the two of them that we were going to have a baby and they'd have a new brother or sister. Josh, being the elder and just entering his teens, was quite funny. 'Well, what are you having a baby for?' he said. At that age, they don't want to think about their parents having babies and all that involves. (He was a fantastic big brother, though, both the boys were great.)

After that, any feeling I had that we were rushing just evaporated – simply, the thought of not being with Colin was inconceivable. In the same vein, if our lives had been running separately (well, at least, officially), we now wanted to be fully committed to each other and get ready to live as a family. While it had got to the point where Colin was at mine pretty much all the time anyway, he moved in properly shortly before the baby was born.

Now, I'm quite good at being pregnant, I've always thought I'm like an old packhorse – I just have 'em and pop 'em out! But this time around, I developed something called symphysis pubis dysfunction, which I'd never had with the boys. I learnt that a hormone called relaxin makes all your ligaments nice and stretchy for when you give birth so you don't actually dislocate yourself. The problem was that I had too much of it too soon. What it felt like was that my pelvis was in a constant state of disconnecting – that was painful. I had to wear this great big support belt to keep it all together and take very little steps – I was on crutches most of the time. I was really worried about giving birth even though this was my third baby. I thought, if I can't even walk easily, how the hell am I going to push a baby out?

I found out on 17 November 2000, when my millennium baby decided it was time to arrive. I was on the phone to a friend at about half past nine that morning, while Colin had gone out to do the school run with the boys. 'Buggeration, I've wet myself,' I exclaimed – before I realised that of course I hadn't, it was my waters breaking. 'I've got to get off the phone to tell Colin!' I told her, hanging up and dialling. Colin came straight back home and, with the little bag I had packed, off we drove to Southend hospital, just 10 minutes away by car.

Colin, fortunately for me, was very good at staying calm.

'Don't meet trouble halfway,' he used to say, which meant don't anticipate worry or anxiety until you really know you've got something to worry about. He dealt with things as they came along, at that moment. So, he was in the car getting me to hospital and it wasn't in his nature to think what would be happening in two hours – 'Oh, I hope this goes okay.' Whereas I stub my toe and I'm planning the funeral. He was a really good balance to me. Today, I've reverted back to type a little.

In the delivery room it was Colin, me and my lovely friend Jenny, who was very maternal and had wanted to see a baby being born. It was always in the plan that she'd come along. It was so happy in that delivery room, I can't tell you. And then my very old school friend Tracy, whom I hadn't seen for 20 years, walked in. She was a midwife working in the hospital, I discovered.

'Do you mind me being here?' she asked.

'No, of course not, it's brilliant to see you again' – by the time you're on baby number three, your dignity's well and truly out of the window. I was quite sure, too, that Tracy had seen it all before, even if her last memory of me was sharing cheese sandwiches as we bunked off school together! We had a real laugh about our school days and the labour progressed quite normally until, about two or three hours before the baby was delivered, it got so bloody painful that I asked if I could have an epidural.

All my friends know I am a hypochondriac and, true to form, I assumed that if anything could go wrong, it would go wrong for me. Having so embraced the online world, I now suffered from cyber-chondria too! I'd made the mistake of reading about complications with epidurals and was convinced I'd be the person getting a 72-hour headache. But as I hesitated, weighing up the pros and cons, any anxieties became secondary to wanting to be pain-free. I signed the form for the procedure as I approached the end of the second stage of labour and, looking back today, I'm quite glad I did. Epidurals, I found, take away enough of the pain that you suddenly go from really feeling a contraction to the midwife saying, 'Ooh, look, you're having another contraction' and thinking: oh, am I?

Then, at last, my baby was handed to me. 'It's an Amelia,' I blurted out. 'It's an Amelia!' It was so emotional. We'd known she was going to be a girl, but it was the reality of her being there – my first girl. She was lovely, such a pretty little thing: 8lb 13oz, with just a wisp of blonde, downy hair and big blue eyes – a beautiful little girl.

I could see Colin in her immediately – the eyes and eyebrows – and fed her straight away. There are not a lot of things that are primal in life any more, it's all sanitised and packaged up, but this isn't. It hurts and it's messy and all those things, but it's just so joyous. It was so very special, having a baby with somebody I loved, really deeply loved. And Colin was a very emotional person too, he wasn't somebody to hide his feelings. He had tears in his eyes as I handed her to him. In fact, there were tears in the delivery room – from everybody! I don't think he could believe he had created this little thing.

'I never thought it would happen for me, ever,' he once

told me. It was the sort of thing that happened to someone else – anyone else – but not to him.

I, meanwhile, was absolutely high on love. When that baby was handed to me, if you can imagine the euphoria when you fall in love and times that by a gazillion, that heady euphoric rush – it's like a drug for me. In fact, after the births of every single one of my children I didn't sleep for days. I don't sleep much anyway, but after having babies some women want – need – to sleep for days. Not me. You know when you can't eat, can't sleep: I felt this excitement and just wanted to stare at their faces all the time. Oh, and to cap it all, the great thing was that within 48 hours of Amelia arriving my pelvis problems disappeared!

Given that he was used to living on a tidal timetable, I suppose it should have been no surprise that Colin was so brilliant at adapting to another strange schedule: Amelia's. I was doing the feeding, but he was a totally hands-on dad. He got involved with everything, nothing was a problem and he was very considerate to me. I didn't even have to take the baby to the clinic to be weighed. Instead, Colin used to take her down to the fish market and put her in the fish scales used to weigh the catch. He'd come back, delighted, and tell me what the dial read now. 'She's as big as that massive great cod I got!' he joked. It tickled both of us.

That said, it's incredible the chaos a baby brings, and we were no exception. While I'd been doing my freelance work from home for Mark's magazine, I was now pretty flat out looking after the boys and a new baby, so Colin was the main breadwinner. That meant that he did the school run for the first few days before going back to work – no paid leave for the self-employed – then I had to carry on as normal, getting out of the house by eight-thirty to get the boys to school. That alone was like a military operation! And of course his wasn't a Monday-to-Friday job. If the weather was good, he'd work seven days a week; but if it was bad – and sometimes in the winter it could be for two or three weeks on the trot – he couldn't go out and we'd have no income at all. The silver lining was that there were often times when we'd be together during the day when he was off. We'd go for walks, see my parents, go to the park, for drives, swimming, for a bike ride.

In fact, because I didn't drive, throughout every single one of my pregnancies – Amelia in particular – I was riding my bike until virtually the day I gave birth, and then I was back on it with a baby seat attached as soon as my children could sit up. I'm sure that's partly why Amelia was so sociable: terribly smiley, really a happy little baby. People's heads would turn, and they'd chat to her, as she was small to be on the back of a bike, but I had all the appropriate baby gear and I was quite an experienced bike rider who didn't take risks. As for Amelia, she really loved it – I used to be able to hear her chuckling behind me as we went along, especially over bumps in the road.

She went everywhere with Colin, too: the fish market, the scrapyard to get bits for his boat, to see his dad Ken, all the places he hung out. Colin used to take me along to keep him company while he worked away on his boat – it needs a lot of maintenance, a boat – and, as Amelia got bigger, very often he'd take her along too. In fact, Amelia was about nine months old when she first went on a boat. None of us would have had life jackets, I was led by him: he was the expert. And I just felt so safe – nothing could happen to us when we were with him.

That first Christmas all together, Amelia just a few weeks old, was wonderful, spent among our families. My boys had had me to themselves for all that time, but when Amelia came home they were lovely big brothers, very gentle and kind with her. I bought Colin, as a first-time father, a special present from the baby: a lovely locket in old rose gold, inscribed with the date of her birth and the message 'To Daddy, from Amelia'. Inside, I put a photograph of her, and one of me and Colin holding her. He never took it off after that.

'You're my Husband'

'**B**limey, there's loads of people in there,' I whispered, my stomach churning. I smoothed down my dress and tried to stay calm.

Standing outside the church in the glorious sunshine, I was waiting for my cue to walk down the aisle – and fervently hoping I wouldn't fall over in front of the dozens of people gathered there. Lots of people had come to the service who didn't have formal invitations, I could tell, which was absolutely fine with me. In the run-up to our big day, I'd been telling pretty much everyone I'd ran into, 'Oh yes, we're getting married, you can pop along.' And, it seemed, everyone had: the church was packed.

But if it was lovely to know so many friends and well-wishers had come to see me get married, I was nervous, knowing everyone would be looking at me. I was in high shoes, too, which I never wear. Dad was keeping my feet on the ground, telling me, 'Oh for goodness' sake, well we haven't come this far for you to back out now!' Still, he was beaming.

Now, as the music played, it was time to move into the spotlight. I took that first step, and the next, and the next. As heads started turning, cameras flashing, Colin, I knew, was even more nervous than me. He was a shy, private person and it wasn't his style to have loads and loads of people. But he smiled at the altar – he really did. And he looked so handsome in his suit.

The two of us getting married was never a case of Colin getting down on one knee, it was much more natural than that. Once Amelia was born we had been having the conversation – 'Well, if we're going to get married, shall we do it while she's a baby?' – and we knew it was going to happen; it was just a question of when. As it was, Amelia was about 18 months old. But if this makes it sound unromantic, then that couldn't be more wrong: it was such a lovely day.

The wedding was in nearby Westcliff-on-Sea, in a beautiful church called St Saviour's, on 4 May 2002. The official ceremony was the day before, however. We were married by an old friend of mine, Steve, the very youthful-looking minister at my church, Southend Vineyard, in a room there – just me, Colin, the kids and very close friends and family. Steve had seen me grow up – as an adult, but also spiritually – so it was very fitting to have him marry us. I'd met him back in the days when I used to busk. What looked like a typical Essex boy in jeans and trainers told me he'd come to Southend to plant a church, and did I want to join him and sing in it? And that was how the local Vineyard started, just a handful of us in a living room. It's massive now, with a congregation of hundreds. So the marriage service itself felt very much like a register office affair, then we went to my parents' house for some champagne. They were thrilled we were getting married: Colin was fantastic son-in-law material, attentive and kind. They loved him like a son, and he behaved like one.

The reason for the two-day arrangement was that Steve was only licensed to marry us in his church, which was modern – like an office building – while I was really keen to get married in St Saviour's, a big, wonderful, old-fashioned church near the sea. The people there were very kind and let Steve perform the blessing for us, which meant going through the marriage service all over again. So, the fourth was the day I felt we were married, with all the guests coming for a really big, full-on affair. We even put 'May the Fourth be with you' – a nod to the famous *Star Wars* line – on the invitations to make people smile.

It was such a special day. My dress was cream. I knew I couldn't afford to buy a dress from a shop, so instead I and my friend Tina, who's the most amazing dressmaker, had flipped through a wedding magazine together, looking for inspiration.

'I really love that,' I'd said, pausing over one particular photo of a model in bridal gear.

'I'll make that for you,' she said. And she did – a lovely sleeveless satin dress, which I wore with a bright red satin jacket with teardrop sleeves and a matching hat, this funny little concoction that caught my fancy, on my head.

Tina wasn't the only person who helped us out. Because we had such a limited budget, people had been really kind and I called in lots of favours – my musician friends helped put a brass section together and so we had this fantastic horn fanfare as I walked down the aisle, with Josh playing the trombone; while my friend Wendy – a very glamorous woman, a professional singer with a phenomenal voice – sang 'Ave Maria' during the service. Knowing a lot of musicians made it a really fantastic event. And I loved the hymns we chose – beautiful, traditional church music – including 'Eternal Father', which a lot of people know by its famous lyric: 'For those in peril on the sea'.

Amelia, of course, was my flower girl, toddling along in her finery, while my cousin's two grown-up daughters, Sarah and Louise, were bridesmaids, along with the daughter of our best man, Les. Yes, that's the same Les who'd rented me the cottage next door to my beloved fisherman. Having been neighbours, his family were old friends of the Dolbys. We felt it was very fitting to have Les play a key role in our wedding, as without him I might never have met Colin.

We had our reception in a place called the Maritime Room, the lower floor of the Cliffs Pavilion theatre, overlooking the sea and the cliffs. In fact, it was that same theatre where I had been telephoning all those estate agents in desperation, all those years ago. There were 60 people coming for the sit-down wedding breakfast, then 150 for the party in the evening. It had taken a year to pay for it all – every week I'd gone in there with money to pay it off and chip away at the total.

After the church service, Colin and I got there first so we could have photographs taken, and there was this moment – just five minutes or so – when that had been done and we were waiting for other people to arrive, when it was just us. We wandered into the venue and saw how beautifully the tables had been decorated, and all the balloons that my friend Lesley had arranged for us. For wedding favours, we'd made CDs for everybody: 10 songs that were really special to me and Colin, significant for us throughout our relationship. We had a picture of me and him as babies on the front of each album, and as adults on the back. Actually, we thought, that was going to be more long-lasting than a few sugared almonds in a bag. And we'd booked a band, who'd done a good mates rates deal, so with the musicians too it all probably looked a lot more expensive than it was! Holding Colin's hand, I thought, this is going to be such a fantastic day – and it was: marrying this man I loved with all my heart, with all my friends there.

It was one of those glorious May days, which turned into a beautiful evening. The doors were open onto the cliffs, with the sea below, and people were spilling onto the grass outside, children playing in real wedding tradition – it was just magical. For our first dance we had 'our' song, Joni Mitchell's 'My Old Man', a slow acoustic guitar number which my friend Wendy sang. And I remember looking at Colin and thinking, oh, he's my husband. In fact, I kept saying that day, whenever I could, 'my husband', 'my husband'. I really was so pleased to have married him. I loved being his wife. I knew without any doubt that this was supposed to happen. And I also knew, even then, that that day was just the wedding. As much as I was enjoying it, I knew that it was a marriage we were starting. In the same way that people focus on the birth, it's really all about parenthood – as I already knew – and I was looking forward to the years, the life, that lay ahead of us.

For our honeymoon, my parents kindly looked after the kids and paid for us to go to Dublin for five days, staying at the Clarence Hotel – Bono's hotel in fact. We found that out after booking it – we weren't particularly fans of his band, U2. But I'd never stayed in such a lovely place. And we loved Dublin, listening to loads of live music and doing all the touristy things, just hanging out, the two of us. We promised ourselves, too, that we'd go back one day – but we didn't.

You just don't think it's going to be over so fast, just a few years later.

Life as the Dolbys

After the wedding, it was back to normal life, except now I was 'Mrs D', as Colin used to call me, and Amelia was so loved that we were keen to have another child. I soon fell pregnant again, but this time it was not so straightforward. In fact, I had two miscarriages – both between 10 and 12 weeks – before getting through that danger zone a third time. I was so relieved, but it was short-lived.

One of my blood tests came back showing that I had an extremely elevated risk of having a child with Down's syndrome. Now 38, I knew on an abstract level that my age could mean I was more likely to encounter problems, but, in reality, when you get that news it's still a complete shock. Still, I got my head round it and Colin and I made the decision that we were going to keep this baby even if it did have Down's. There wasn't really a discussion to have: we wanted this baby and we were committed to it. I did go to hospital in London to have amniocentesis – the needle through the belly, into the fluid in the womb, to test whether the baby did have Down's or not. But the reason I'd agreed to the tests wasn't so that we could terminate the pregnancy if the result was positive for Down's, it was because we needed to know what to expect, so that we could be prepared, find local support groups and gear ourselves up for it emotionally.

The tests, however, came back as negative for Down's – but what they did find was a problem with my umbilical cord. As it was explained to me, you've got two strands: one taking nutrients and oxygen to the baby, another taking it all away. I, however, only had one, so it was doing both jobs. That wasn't a big deal when the baby inside me was still small, but it was a problem as he grew and put more strain on the one strand. I had to go into hospital every couple of weeks to check enough oxygen was reaching the baby and I wasn't allowed to go over my due date in case he got too big. So, he was induced in hospital in Southend on 20 December 2004, weighing in at 7lb 13oz.

We called him Liam. Colin hadn't been holding out for a boy or a girl – he revelled in all aspects of fatherhood: the girls, the boys, the stepkids, he loved it all – but he was thrilled to be a father once again. Baby Liam, meanwhile, turned out to be the spit of Colin in so many ways. Today, Liam is the closest you'd get to meeting Colin: he's so much like his dad in his character – happy-go-lucky – and he's the double of him as well, a mini-Colin, down to his beautiful brown eyes.

With four children between us, it certainly wasn't easy, though. For the first year of Liam's life, we had moved from the fisherman's cottage to an upstairs flat in Leigh, where we spent a couple of years before we moved to our current, family-sized house – funnily enough, on the road where I'd grown up. So, for a time, the six of us were in a three-bedroom place, and Liam had to share with us – and, of all the children, he was the one we had the most problems with at night! With my fourth, I just assumed I would take it all in my stride. But he was just relentless; he cried and cried and cried, keeping everyone awake.

Colin would be totally sleep-deprived and having to get up at stupid o'clock for work; I would be sitting sobbing with exhaustion, having to get the other kids to school the next day – Amelia, too, now she'd reached school age. Liam, meanwhile, would sleep, cry, sleep and cry: it was like setting your alarm clock every 15 minutes. Just as well I didn't know then that I wouldn't have a full night's sleep until Liam was seven! At least by then, I knew what the problem was, because when he started talking he could finally tell me: he had terrible, terrible night cramps in his feet. And, of course, when he got older he could say, 'My feet hurt, my feet hurt' and I'd rub them until the pain went away – but there was a long period when we didn't know what was wrong.

Colin, in particular, was badly affected by the sleep deprivation, as recharging after a day's hard graft was proving almost impossible. At least I was more able to catch up on my sleep – snatch half an hour in the day here and there, and it's incredible what a difference that can make – but out on the water he had to be very alert, and do a very physical job after months and months of broken nights. Still, we survived it and loads of parents have to go through the same thing.

And, if the nightly ordeals weren't pleasant, Colin just relished everything else. He carried little Amelia like she was a great big fish under one arm, turning up at the school gates with her wriggling around. He'd make the mums in the playground roar with laughter. Once Liam was big enough too, it would be one child under each arm and 'Out we go, kids!' It makes me smile to think of it. But, you see, being a fisherman wasn't just a job. It was a way of life that coloured every part of him – and it nourished, rather than drained him.

After a long day on the water, he would be exhausted – he'd be out of the house for 12 hours or more. But, if he was finishing work at a reasonable time, he would always pop in to see his dad, have a cup of tea; pick the kids up from school. And he'd come home and launch straight back into family life. Everything he did was super-fast: while I'd linger over the housework, break off midway through the hoovering to have a cup of tea, Colin would do everything as if he was being timed. He got it from working on the boat: as he couldn't afford an extra pair of hands to help him, he had to work at a rapid pace. 'I've got all this to do,' I'd sometimes say as I faced a pile of clearing-up. And if I headed upstairs for a moment, when I'd come back down it would all have been cleared away.

He wasn't someone to look for 'Colin time'. And he recharged by spending time with the children. So he'd get involved with bathing the kids, we'd have dinner, laugh about what the kids had been up to. As a toddler, Liam didn't talk for a long time and when he did decide to start he had a funny little language of his own – it wasn't proper English that he spoke; he'd made it up himself. So, shoes were 'fishfahs'; bananas were 'la-las'; and there were loads of other things I forget now, but for almost everything you could think of he had an alternative word. I'm really upset that I can't remember, because the only other person who could remember isn't here.

Colin loved seeing the children develop their own personalities, they were so different. As a little girl, Amelia had very intense friendships with people. She liked one-to-ones – maybe it was because it was such a busy house; she quite enjoyed the intimacy of small groups of friends. And she was – is – super-organised. If I asked Amelia to cook me a roast dinner she could do it. Organising is her thing and she's been like that since she was very small, getting her clothes out ready for the next day. She loves structure, routine. 'Where does it come from?' Colin and I would ask each other. Not me, I admit. Colin was organised – you have to be if you run your own business – but she was on another level. Meanwhile, Liam was just chaos. And while from an early age Amelia loved colour, design, was choosy about her outfits, Liam didn't care; I could put him in anything. He just wanted to get out and kick a ball – very much like Colin.

He was pleased about Liam's date of birth – the 20th of the 12th – which wasn't as mad as it sounded. Just before our son was born, it had been announced that if London won the bid for the 2012 Olympics, everyone born on 20/12 that year would participate in the Games in some way. So, on each birthday, as Liam grew bigger, he'd get a card from Sebastian Coe, who led the organising committee, reminding him that he was going to be taking part. Every year Colin, who liked sport, would say, 'Oh, I wonder what will happen at the Olympics.' It was so exciting for them both: our little boy was turning out to be very athletic, always active, running around. He could ride a bike before he was three – so young that people were astonished when they saw him cycling.

Colin and Amelia had their shared interests too. The pair of them had watched *Chitty Chitty Bang Bang* together about 500 times – they just loved that film. When the stage version came to London, we couldn't afford for us all to go, and Colin had never been to a West End show, so I said, 'You take her.' Amelia, being just a little thing, was terrified when the Child Catcher came on stage, Colin told me afterwards, hiding under the seat! Still, she absolutely loved the rest of it. When they came back, he was exhausted – it wasn't his world, the city. I'm so glad he took her, now, that she's got that memory; it would have been so easy for me to have taken her.

Life, really, was pretty good: Colin tending to be the calm at the centre of the storm. One time, I remember, we were at a chain restaurant – a Hungry Horse, or similar – with the kids, and I don't know whether I was already annoyed with him about something trivial. But when we sat down and he ordered his steak very well done, I got a real bee in my bonnet.

'Why are you having it well done?' I asked him. 'You won't be able to taste it!'

'Well, I like it well done,' said Colin. 'I'm paying for it so I'm having it how I want.' Which of course he could, but for some reason – maybe the wind was blowing in the wrong direction – it irritated me.

'You're not in bloody Torremolinos now!' I said. And off I stomped.

Outside, I suddenly remembered I didn't have any money on me to get home. I was too proud to go back in, but we were miles away from Leigh. Of course, for some that would have been the moment to go back into the restaurant, cool down and have a nice meal. But not me. I'll have to bunk the fares, I thought – me, a fortysomething mother of four! So I got on the train – and I promptly went the wrong way. I couldn't even phone Colin as I had no phone credit, so again I had to try and bunk the fare back to my family. By the time I got off and returned to the pub, they were all finishing their meal. I had to go in, really sheepish and by now so hungry I'd have gladly wolfed down the most cremated of T-bones.

I totally saw the funny side by that point. We all roared with laughter. The kids talked about it for a long time afterwards: 'Remember that time Mum walked out of the restaurant and got the train in the wrong direction? And then she had to come back.'

I never minded – I loved listening to everyone reminiscing over our young family's history, that we were building up our funny little traditions. Colin, for instance, always liked his Hawaiian shirts. It became a bit of a family joke: if you buy Colin a shirt it's got to be very loud. Goodness knows why, it wasn't his character at all, but he just liked those shirts. And I think he played up to it a bit as well, because we all started trying to outdo each other, seeing who could buy him the loudest, most ridiculous shirt of all. He'd unwrap a present at Christmas, and some swirling pink and yellow horror would be revealed, much to his delight. It really made us all laugh. I'd get him 'proper' presents too: one year I paid for him to go on an adventure survival weekend with a good friend of his, which he loved. And every year, on his birthday, 28 August, we'd have a party. 'It doesn't matter what the weather's been like, it's going to be good,' Colin would say – and, often, he was right. It started the first year we were together and got bigger and bigger, with all our friends round in the garden.

We'd have lovely family times on holiday, too. Until I met Colin, I hadn't had a holiday since I was a kid, not really. I'd had one week in Malta with the boys, when they were three and seven, and that was it. With Colin, we didn't go away every year and when we did, we just went to cheap places like Haven resorts, caravan parks – what we could afford and reach by his car. I'd be doing what I did at home, but in a different location, it did occur to me at times, when I was washing up or making dinner! Still, we'd be recharged, able to spend time together without Colin having to get out of bed before dawn or worry about the tide times.

We never went abroad together as a family, and I wish we had. It was the expense, of course. In the July of 2008, I did go away with the children to my cousin's daughter

Louise's wedding in Valence in the south of France – Louise who had been one of my bridesmaids. For me, that was one of the most wonderful times. The whole family was there, and everything was paid for except for the flights, but even then money was tight. Colin wouldn't take the time off work because it was the height of summer; he was all too aware that winters are so lean for fishermen, he couldn't afford to. Sometimes, I knew, he would go out and not even come back with enough of a catch to cover the cost of his diesel.

Still, I begged him to come with me – and I really wish he had. He would have done if he'd known what was ahead, of course. Later on, I remember thinking: why the hell didn't you come with me? We'd never been abroad together before.

In August that same year we went to Weymouth, and Colin could come that time. That was one of the loveliest holidays we had. We stayed in a caravan park and went out every day exploring the Dorset coast, under big blue skies and glorious sunshine. The sands are beautiful and we were there during the time of a big world sand-sculpting competition. The stuff they created was incredible – strange creatures and buildings twisting out of the sands; when do you wake up one morning and decide, 'I think I'll do that!' The kids loved it too: we took two children from Amelia's class and a boy who played with Liam a lot as well. And that was our last family holiday.

I'm glad we had that. I treasure those memories.

Storm on the Horizon

Monday, 10 November 2008 fell six weeks before Christmas, seven days before Amelia's eighth birthday. Remembering those events, my life with Colin feels as if it were a hundred years ago – and, at the same time, as if it were yesterday. People might imagine that in the moments before a tragedy, those close to the victim may get a sense of danger, some sort of premonition, alarm bells ringing. I didn't.

That morning, Colin was dropping Amelia off at school and Liam at his pre-school, then heading off to work for a day's fishing. Today, he was 'weeding' – raking the seabed for white weed, what looks like pale sea ferns. He'd bag it up and sell it on and it would be dyed and used in aquariums and for home decoration, of all things. It lasts pretty much for ever.

A lot of fishermen turn to weeding in the winter months when the fish have migrated elsewhere. Colin had even made his own massive rakes in his workshop to collect the stuff. Each as big as a sofa, they were like giant versions of the afro combs you see: metal, with big spaces between the teeth. He'd drag them along the seabed behind his boat and they'd come up full of what looked like feathery carrot tops. But white weed is not actually a plant at all: it's got more in common with coral. A lot of people are quite allergic to it, Colin among them. There was something about the stuff that made him asthmatic, so that every time he was out weeding he would have to take an inhaler with him. Still, needs must.

'It won't be a long day,' he said. Then he checked the weather his usual way – he went into the garden and looked at the trees, to see which way the wind was blowing. He made sure to check the shipping forecast, too, and got his gear together with his usual speedy efficiency, rushing around. Winter was definitely setting in, I thought: as the days grew shorter, there was a real nip in the air.

As he left, I kissed Colin goodbye and gave his bum a playful squeeze.

'Don't go to work, Cobbs, stay home and ravish me instead,' I teased him.

'Someone has to pay for Christmas,' he replied. And off he went.

He should have stayed. I wish he'd stayed.

The house uncharacteristically quiet with everyone gone, I tidied away the breakfast things – mealtimes could be organised chaos with the six of us – and did a bit of house-work. Soon, though, I headed upstairs to the computer. Whenever I had time to myself, I'd try and get on with some of the promotional work I was doing with local musicians, making a bit to put by for a holiday for us all, or some other treat for the family. I was always all too aware that I didn't have that long to myself even on a school day – you drop the kids off, and you've only got three or four hours, tops, before you've got to go and pick them up again.

Work aside, that morning there was something else on my mind: Christmas was just around the corner and there was so much to do, what with the four children to shop for and all our in-laws and relatives. I was keen to get on top of it all. Soon, I made myself a fresh cup of coffee, opened up a new webpage and started browsing through shopping sites. Colin had lent me his debit card, so I could get on with buying some presents for the kids online.

It was midday – and I was still upstairs shopping for presents – when the noise outside caught my attention. I looked out of the window: rain was lashing down against the pane and the sky was dark. The weather had just turned, gone from fairly clear to appalling. You'd call it a squall – heavy rain and wind, really fierce – the sort of wind that can blow you over. I stayed at the computer, glad to be cosy inside on a day like this. But a few minutes later a crash came: some tiles had blown off the roof. Bugger. That wasn't going to be cheap.

I gave Colin a call, as I knew he had the phone number of a friend of his who was a roofer. 'Cobbs, the storm's taken the tiles off. Can you text me the number of your mate and I'll organise to get the roof done?'

His words came in a rush. 'The weather's terrible! I can't talk to you now, darlin', I can't talk – I'm trying to lash down everything on the boat. It's awful out here.'

'Okay,' I said, 'no problem.'

He said, 'I'll see you in a couple of hours – I'll be home to take you to the party.'

This was a birthday party for a little girl who was at pre-school with Liam. Her mum and I had become friendly, so she had invited both Amelia and Liam to the party in the church hall after school. Colin and I were going to leave the kids there for a couple of hours and the plan was that we'd go into Southend to do some Christmas shopping together while we had the chance. I was looking forward to it, getting in the festive mood already.

I grabbed myself some lunch, and stayed at the computer: Liam was being dropped off from pre-school soon, by a friend's mum. For a while I lost myself in the task before me; then Liam arrived home. 'Hello, gorgeous boy!' I said, unwrapping this small figure from his wet coat. 'What have you been up to today?' And so it was back into the usual bustle of family life.

I wasn't worried when it got to three o'clock, when Colin was due back to pick me up, and there was no sign of him. He always warned me, 'Never set your watch by a fisherman.' I tried to reach him on his mobile and it came up as unobtainable. Phone signals are often patchy at sea, I knew.

But it did mean a change in my plans. This is a pain, I thought: I'm going to have to go and do the school run to get Amelia in torrential rain. I didn't drive, and the storm that had sprung up showed no sign of abating. As I stepped outside to see how bad it was, the force of the raindrops made my face smart and I almost lost my footing in the wind. I was running late for Amelia by then too, as it was more than a 15-minute walk to her school. She'll be out by about quarter past, I reminded myself – I'm going to have to call a taxi. A few minutes later, one arrived to pick up me and Liam and, as the driver kept the engine running outside, I rushed into the school, grabbed Amelia and went straight to the party.

As Colin still hadn't turned up, I stayed to help with the kids and games – pass the parcel, musical statues – while Amelia and Liam ran around, excited to be among all their friends. So it was after four when I pulled out my phone to try Colin again. I had about 10 missed calls from his sister Wendy, I saw. That wasn't usual.

Something has happened to their dad, Ken, I thought immediately.

My stomach churning, I stepped outside the church hall where the party was still in full swing, into the rain lashing down. Holding my coat over my head to try to protect my phone, I called Wendy back. She was near-hysterical, crying down the phone. 'Colin's boat – his boat's not back,' she was saying. 'Colin hasn't come back, Jane!'

Lost

'Well, I know he hasn't come back,' I said, quite matter-of-fact. 'He was supposed to take me to this bloody party. Don't worry about it, Wendy, you know what he's like: he always says, don't set your watch by a fisherman. You know this more than anyone.'

Her call wasn't triggering any panic in me. I remember, so clearly, feeling bewildered by what seemed such an over-reaction to poor timekeeping, as I tried to explain that Colin was often late home. Now that I knew nothing had happened to Ken, my initial alarm subsided. I just wanted to reassure her and get back indoors out of the downpour.

'No,' Wendy told me, slowing her words. 'You don't understand, Jane. His boat's not back. We can't see his boat. His boat hasn't come back to the mooring. We've called the coastguard.'

My whole body went cold. As she said it, I just knew. At that moment, with the same absolute certainty I'd known that Colin was the man I'd marry, I knew I would never ever see him again. Beyond logic or reason, I just knew. A terrible fear – pure dread – filled me.

Because he always returned to the same mooring, out by the pier, if you were standing on the seafront you could see his boat when he was back from fishing. When Wendy told me his boat wasn't back, I knew that meant it wasn't on the mooring and it wasn't visible anywhere else. Colin hadn't been busy loading his catch into the trailer, dropping it off at the fish merchant's, got talking to someone, all his usual routine. He hadn't come back at all. That could only mean one thing: his boat had sunk.

What I would learn later is that, as the weather deteriorated, the winds had gusted up to Force 8 amid rough seas. At about a quarter to one, Colin had radioed his father, onshore, to say he was returning to the mooring because the weather was getting worse.

But he had failed to show up. It was Ken who, desperately worried, had called Thames Coastguard at three o'clock. As the storm raged, he had gone up in his mobility scooter to the top of the road to look out to sea. I still picture it: this old man, in the pouring rain, looking for his son. To this day, I can't think of it without wanting to cry.

It's impossible to predict how one responds to a crisis. Before that day, if I'd had to place a bet, I would have probably given good odds on my becoming very emotional and uncontrolled, but the opposite happened. At that moment of impact my thinking became crystal-clear, very ordered – immediately, I knew I had to make as many calls as possible before the party ended to find out what was going on, hold it together, and get the children away.

I stayed outside the hall, on my mobile phone. The rain was still teeming down, like shards of glass. I tried Colin's phone again, just as Wendy had tried him. Unobtainable.

I got the number for the coastguard, where a man told me, 'We're out looking for the boat, we're going to send a rescue team.' I left my mobile number so I could be updated.

And I phoned my friend Angee. 'I think something's happened to Colin,' I said, with an unnatural steadiness, 'his boat went missing in the storm.' It was instinct – I just wanted her, felt safe with her. She's fantastic, Angee. A true English eccentric, I know why she's such a good nurse: she's wonderful in a crisis – rock-solid, practical and a really lovely, big-hearted woman. She asked me where I was. Later I learnt that she was at the bank, trying to negotiate a mortgage. 'F— the mortgage!' she'd shouted. 'My friend's in need.' She didn't drive either so she jumped in a taxi to join me at the church hall.

I felt, strangely, as if everything was slowing down: as though events were unfolding more gradually than they normally did. I was starting to feel somehow removed from everything: as though I was both a participant and an observer. I'd be experiencing great waves of cold fear, deep, deep dread, and thinking, this is interesting.

Perhaps that was shock; perhaps the human brain is so incredible that, during a time of trauma, the victim experiences the event in slow motion to allow them crucial thinking time. I still don't know. The brain really does some odd things in times of great pressure.

But I was thinking fast. I couldn't tell the children anything, not yet, not while I myself was still finding out what had happened. The best thing was for them to go to my brother's, I decided. Robin had grown up to be an osteopath and still lived locally; he'd met a lovely woman, Siobhan, in the office and they'd had a little girl together. He'd always been there at the end of the phone. I had become close to Siobhan, too – a striking Glaswegian woman, full of wisdom. I could rely on them.

I got a message to them, explaining what was happening. Angee must have phoned them, as I was trying to get more information from the coastguard and the police.

Then I held it together as Amelia and Liam came out of the party – 'Have you had a nice time?' – and gave Angee the key so she could head back with them to the house by taxi, to sort their clothes and things out before my brother picked them up.

I carried on making calls.

At one point, one of the other children's dads came out of the party to have a cigarette. 'What are you doing out here?' he asked me. 'The weather's awful.'

'My husband's a fisherman, he's out in it, we can't find his boat.'

He said, 'Oh dear.' He didn't understand the significance.

Then, after that initial mental clarity in the first minutes of shock, my memories get so very hazy. It's like a big black void.

I don't remember how I got back to the house, I don't remember when my brother and my sister-in-law arrived, but I do know we pretended that it was a big adventure and the children were going to have a sleepover on a school night at their cousins'.

'You children are so lucky,' I told them, 'because tonight you're going to have a sleepover at Uncle Robin's.'

'But we've got school tomorrow!' they chorused.

'Yeah, life's too short for school sometimes,' I told them.

'Well, why are we going to Uncle Robin's?' they asked.

'Well, why not?' I said – really just making it like an adventure. And they thought it was brilliant. They didn't question why too much, either, probably too worried I'd change my mind.

So, my brother took the kids back to his house and Siobhan stayed with me.

More people arrived. A man called Garry from the police, who must have been in his early thirties and told me he was our family liaison officer; Stephen the minister from my current church, Leigh Road Baptist Church. Now my living room was full but I felt very alone – and numb. All these people were there and it seemed to stay like that for ages.

I was functioning: I answered questions, made cups of tea. My older boys had their own lives by then – Josh was in Berlin, working as a musician; Henry was still at home, but was out that day in Southend with his friends – so I had to phone them both. My parents had to be told. So I had things to do.

I didn't tell Amelia what had happened that first night because, as Garry said, 'We don't know what's happened. We might find him, he might be in the boat, he might have sought shelter in another vessel – or something.'

That evening it was all over the TV news – I had to turn it off.

The rescue effort was focusing on the area of Colin's last known position: just after one o'clock that afternoon, his boat had disappeared off the radar. I knew what that could signal: that it had gone under. But the hope was that Colin might have been thrown from his trawler, or been sheltering in a nearby boat.

The search was co-ordinated from Shoebury coastguard tower, a little way further up the coastline. It looks out over a dark hump in the water that you can see from shore: a wreck of a Second World War floating harbour. That's where the search focused: Colin had apparently told Ken he was near there as he was heading back home and it matched the last radar trace for his vessel.

As night fell so many people – friends and strangers – were out on the seafront, walking up and down, looking for him. The lifeboats were out, a hovercraft, the sky lighting up with flares fired to illuminate the water and help the searchers. An RAF helicopter swept low over the water, close to the waves. And the other fishermen were incredible, every single one of them: they even took their boats out in dangerous waters looking for Colin. Some are members of the RNLI, so were part of the lifeboat crew itself.

At home, we prayed for his speedy rescue. But it was so treacherous that the searchers were now risking their own lives in the strong winds and rough seas. As the hours passed with no news of Colin, Garry didn't pull any punches. 'The search is going to have to stop for the night,' he said.

Angee was combative, fighting my corner. 'Well, why's it going to stop,' she asked, 'he's still missing, isn't he?'

But I was very practical. 'They can't carry on, can they?' I said. 'It's dangerous for them.'

I remember thinking: there is no point in being hysterical, what is that going to achieve? What is the point? I'm not going to be able to be effective. I don't even know if I cried.

That was difficult for me afterwards. Because, for a long time after losing Colin, I stayed practical. And I had this terrible guilt about what that meant, that maybe I didn't love Colin, not properly. I just thought, why am I not falling apart? Of course, the pain came afterwards – and how it came – but at the time I didn't know about shock, how it anaesthetises you. For those few hours of the immediate aftermath, I was almost stunned.

The Aftermath

It was in the 48 hours after Wendy's call that we slowly came to the terrible truth: Colin was gone. I'd known it emotionally from the very start; but it took time for me to come to it intellectually.

After that first night, the search party went back out at five in the morning. Robin brought the kids home and Amelia went to school as normal. I phoned her teachers to let them know what had happened, to warn them to be careful what they said. Much of what unfolded over those days is blurry or blank to me: I've impressions and a sense of how I was feeling more than a clear memory of what I was doing. Did I sleep? Surely, I must have – perhaps exhaustion seized me. At moments, I know, I was calm. Then suddenly I'd be gripped by a pain so raw, so unbearable it would leave me gasping.

I will never see Colin again, *I will never see him again.*

I'd compare it to when a woman's in labour. When you're in the grip of a contraction, it's impossible to remember being free of pain; in fact it's impossible to focus on anything other than enduring the agony. When the pain passed, I would wonder why I hadn't coped better with it, feeling that, when it hit me again, it wouldn't be as bad. I'd be wrong.

And so the hours passed: Garry, Siobhan, Angee, a couple of other close friends, coming and going. At one point I came downstairs – I'd been having a shower upstairs – and there was a stranger sitting in my living room.

'I'm here to help.'

I looked at this burly bloke and thought, what? 'Well, who the hell are you?' I said, not really taking it in properly. 'What are you doing here?'

'I'm Tim Jenkins, I'm from the Fishermen's Mission. I'm here to say, obviously, that we're sorry and to see what support you need.'

He had a Welsh accent, I noticed. I'd never heard of the Fishermen's Mission, didn't know what they did – and told him so.

'My job is to support families in hardship,' he explained, 'and when there's a fisherman missing, I'm here to support in any way you need.'

So I let him stay. At the time, I didn't really understand what he did and I understood what our needs were even less. But he did say, 'We can pray with you, whatever you need, to support you,' and I said, 'Yes, I'm a Christian.'

I didn't know it then, but from that point on he wouldn't really leave my side.

I faced each piece of news as it came, as the authorities built up a picture of what had happened. Garry was very good at gauging what to tell me and when: he quickly realised I didn't want any information glossed over, I didn't want it broken to me in a 'kindly' voice; I just wanted – needed – the facts.

Colin's boat, we heard, had disappeared off the radar at the same time as a powerful gust of wind was recorded by the Met Office. I was told the moment it had happened: two minutes past one, that afternoon. That surely wasn't more than an hour after I'd last spoken to him on the phone, I thought, after the tiles had blown off the roof. In my heart of hearts I knew the timing couldn't be a coincidence – that, out there on the rough seas, we'd lost track of Colin just as the storm reached its worst.

But no one would really say that – not in so many words.

Some of my friends, who were there supporting me, tried to help. 'Don't give up hope, Jane, you don't know,' they urged me. I remember someone telling me: 'Colin might have taken shelter in another boat and just not been able to reach us yet.' But I couldn't shake the cold, sick feeling that consumed me. I checked with Garry: the radar data had picked up that there were no other vessels in the vicinity of Colin's boat, so he couldn't have swum to anything. We knew, too, that if he had fallen into the water, he had four minutes until cold-water shock set in; he didn't wear a life jacket.

When I put it all together... I knew what it meant, just as I'd known since I'd first got the call from Colin's sister to say his boat wasn't back.

Then came news from the coastguards: using sonar, something had been found on the seabed in the area that they'd been searching. They couldn't be sure that it was

Colin's boat until they brought it up, but it was likely. It's hard to say how I took this: looking back, I have a sense of the information coming in dribs and drabs, none of it good. But at this stage, it wasn't as if there was some moment of clarity when someone official suddenly announced what we all knew in our hearts: that Colin was gone.

There's a process that kicks into gear when something like this happens. I had to be interviewed by the police, formally. They wanted to know about Colin's state of mind. There were so many questions: what was he wearing? Had he been depressed? Were there any money troubles? Who were his friends? Did I have anything with his DNA on – a toothbrush, a hairbrush? Could I find some photographs? I knew they had a job to do and I found it oddly comforting to be tasked with a to-do list. At least I was contributing something, rather than just sitting about. I had to go through loads of phone numbers recorded by his phone network, Vodafone, too: who was this, who was that, did I recognise this number? We all knew that Colin was at the bottom of the sea, but without a body it was a missing person's investigation and they had to follow a procedure. And I knew that; there was no point in saying, 'Why the bloody hell are we having to go through this?'

But people got very indignant about that on my behalf. I knew that the police weren't doing it to be horrible to me, but it was hours of questioning, working on Colin's relationships with the various people in his life, whom he'd been speaking to. 'Did I know this number or a number like it?' There was one number on his phone, with a northern dialling code, and I didn't recognise it, I remember. I think they put it down to a misdial in the end because it didn't go anywhere, but that was the level of detail they were going into.

And there was the media to deal with. Odd as it sounds, I wrote a press release. I knew the papers would be in touch and I didn't want to speak to anyone. I called the editor of the *Echo*, our local daily paper. I knew him well because of all the music promotion work I had been doing, getting my acts into his pages.

'Please don't write anything Martin, because I haven't told the children,' I begged him.

'I can hold off for a day, Jane, but it's news – you know I've got to run it.'

And I did, I knew how it worked: if he didn't run a story someone else, with no link to me or Colin or our community, would. But I needed that breathing space he gave me, and I was grateful.

The local radio reporters were brilliant as well. I spoke to someone who said they could wait for 12 hours. Really, the regional media were very good to me, but they had to run the story eventually and I knew they had to. I wanted, also, to be in control of something, because everything was so completely out of control. So that's how I ended up sitting on my computer, writing a press release, just as I had in work mode for the bands I helped promote. It felt right. I know it sounds a weird thing to say, but I just felt like I was in control of what was being said. I wrote up what had happened, that Colin was missing, and I put in a quote from me, everything.

I sent it to the *Echo*, the *Leigh Times*, the local *Advertiser*. Maybe they thought it was weird, me doing it. Well, Martin didn't. He knew me; he understood. I just didn't want anyone making things up or reporting inaccuracies; but I didn't want people phoning me up and having to go through it all again and again. And it did make it easier. There was tons written; radio and national TV, too. The *Daily Mirror* ran a story: 'Fisherman is lost at sea in storm chaos'. 'A fisherman was missing last night after being swept off his trawler in bad weather as heavy rain and gale-force winds battered Britain,' it began. I didn't need to read any more.

I hated the thought of other people knowing the news before the children, but I knew it didn't really matter in the scheme of things. I was right to send out that release, I felt sure.

But if I sound as if I had it all together, that's not really the case. Tim from the Fishermen's Mission has reminded me of some of what happened, and how he came to be involved. One of his colleagues, a fundraiser, had been browsing through the internet and saw on one of the fishing websites that there was a search on for Colin. He'd texted Tim to alert him, and he'd immediately started phoning round contacts. Eventually he'd got hold of Ken, and arranged to go and see him, and it was Ken who then put him in touch with me.

I was, he says, all over the place, not knowing what was happening – at the start hoping, of course, that Colin would be found, but – it seemed to him – even then knowing in my heart of hearts that he wasn't going to be found. Tim could do little more than sit with me, offering the silent support of his presence. But he was able to help in a small way, able to get the immediate pressures facing us in Colin's absence: how to keep the household afloat at a time of the year when we were really strapped for cash anyway, given that it was winter and not the season for fishing. 'Well, first of all, let me say, straight away, don't worry about that,' Tim told me. 'I haven't got it with me today, but I'll come back and see you tomorrow and I'll have cash that I can give you. So the immediate financial worry is out of the way.'

And he stayed with me well into the afternoon that first day he appeared on my doorstep, for four or five hours. One by one my friends went, Garry, the police liaison officer, went, and he told me a bit more about the support he could give. As well as tackling the immediate – food on the table for the kids and for me, even if I didn't feel like eating – Tim explained how he'd be accessing some other grants for longer-term help too. As well as the Fishermen's Mission, he was an agent for various other maritime charities; it's very joined-up in that respect. I wasn't really holding onto the information – I don't remember what he told me that day – but I do still have a sense of him as a comforting, reassuring presence. So, I was functioning: talking, getting things done, keeping things together. What I found is that, when you're in the initial state of grief, you're not operating on a deep emotional level all the time.

But then the next wave of grief would approach: I'd feel it coming, growing, increasing in intensity and there'd be nothing I could do to avoid it. I'd be gripped by this terrible feeling of panic – go absolutely cold inside. I can only describe it as a wave of terror. It was this bone-deep knowledge that everything was wrong, in a way I could barely comprehend, and would never be right again. So that was how it was for me: unpredictable, unavoidable waves of pain between brief, but cruelly hopeful, periods of respite.

And throughout it all, for much of the time, I'd feel as if I was observing the whole thing almost as an out-of-body experience: 'Oh, that's interesting' – just oddly detached. I was very rarely totally immersed in it. I don't know whether that's your mind protecting you from the grief. Those moments when I was totally immersed in my own pain were terrifying, because I didn't even know how I would find the motivation to take the next breath. I was overwhelmed by the agony of loss.

What I couldn't stand was that my children had to face this too. Garry advised me not to tell them that Colin was dead because we didn't know – not for sure. Garry was very professional, very boundaried, but very kind. I trusted his advice. When the kids came home that day – Amelia back from school, Liam from pre-school – I broke it to them as gently as I could. 'Daddy is missing. We can't find him at the moment. We don't know where his boat is at the moment.'

'Is he dead?' Amelia asked.

'He might be.' I couldn't shield her from it. 'He might be.'

I really felt I had to answer any questions they had honestly. Planting that seed – 'he might be dead' – was, of course, traumatic, but the seed was there. Maybe, I hoped, that would mean it would be a little bit gentler when the worst came to fruition.

But it was very hard.

On Wednesday morning we woke up to more newspaper headlines. *The Times* ran a story, again focusing on the terrible weather conditions: 'Freak tornado leaves a trail of damage,' it read. 'The Met Office confirmed that fronts over south-east England had created the conditions for a tornado. Yesterday Colin Dolby, 47, a trawler skipper, was missing after his 40ft boat disappeared from radar screens in gales in the Thames Estuary, and a 44-year-old Spanish fisherman died after he was lashed by a snapped cable in 50mph winds off the Scilly Islands.'

Then police divers reached the boat, which had been located on the seabed: about a mile from shore, in some 70 feet of water. We were all expecting Colin to be found in the wheelhouse, which housed the wheel he used to steer the boat. Divers attached chains to the boat and it was slowly winched up from the seabed. But Colin wasn't in the wheelhouse; nor was he down in the boat's cabin. The boat was taken to dry dock at Gravesend in Kent to be emptied of water and for a final check of the engine room, which is deeper inside the boat. Still nothing. Essex police were now describing my husband as officially 'lost at sea'.

Now I had to tell the children – Amelia then seven, Liam just three – that their dad was dead. I had to explain that his body hadn't been found. And because it hadn't been found and the water was so cold, there was very little chance he was alive and that their daddy was dead.

That was terrible. To have to expose your children to pain in that way goes against every instinct you have as a mother. Seeing them tortured with pain and not being able to relieve it is agony. 'As long as I handle it properly, they will be okay,' I kept telling myself. 'They will be okay. We will be okay.' I knew that they would take their cues from me so I was not going to fall apart; I wouldn't become hysterical or leave someone else to deliver the news. I would not let them down. I remember my dad was there, too, Siobhan, Angee, maybe Stephen from church, maybe Tim from the Mission. I was just focused on the kids.

But Liam – he was only three. He really didn't understand. He just said, 'Can we still go swimming tomorrow?'

Amelia, being older, grasped more of the significance of what I was telling them. She understood as much as a seven-year-old has the capacity to understand. We used to go to church together. 'You haven't prayed hard enough, you haven't prayed hard enough!' she told me. I knew that, however hard we prayed, it wasn't going to bring him back. But I said, 'Do you want to pray?' and we did.

You shouldn't have to tell that to your children. It's a really horrible thing to do. That was the worst. But they didn't really understand then, not really.

Survival

The next day, I did take them swimming – just as we'd planned before Colin was lost. Sarah, who'd been my bridesmaid and had been down visiting her grandmother – my aunt – came round. She was really young then, just in her early twenties, but mature for her years: she was doing her training to be a doctor at the time. 'I want to take the children swimming after school,' I said. 'Do you mind if you come with me?' It was the last thing I fancied doing. But I just had this thought that if I didn't get them in water soon it was something that potentially could become a problem for them later on. It's going to be difficult enough, I thought, I don't want to add any issues to the equation if I can help it. And I've always liked being in water – it's like being in the womb, I think, we're all water babies really.

Yes, it was a surreal thing to do. But having children, I was learning, means that your love for them is greater than your own pain. Only just. But enough, just a fraction enough, to drag me through those difficult early months and help me put one foot in front of the other. For it was those acts of having to get up for them, having to make a packed lunch, feed them when they came home – even though I might not feel like doing all these normal things – that I credit with keeping me normal, on some sort of track. Yes, at times, dealing with my small children – and the pain and rage of my older boys – was exhausting, but it helped keep me going. Because otherwise, I know, I could have just descended into blackness and hopelessness. I found the responsibility of lone parenthood utterly exhausting. I longed for someone to offer to take the children away for hours so I could just lie on the bed with a duvet over me, breathing in the scent of Colin's clothes. I was on autopilot, functioning, but not really present in anything I did.

There were limits to my endurance. I didn't go into the school playground for about three weeks. I couldn't face doing the school run. I just did not want to have to talk about it to anybody outside of my bubble: Angee, my brother, my sister-in-law, Tim. And, although they'd been strangers to me just a few days earlier, I became very attached to Garry and Tim. I felt bound to them: they were my security blanket. When somebody's been through something with you – maybe not for them in the same way, it being their job – there's a bond. With Tim, also, we had our shared faith, and we'd pray together quite often, with whomever else was around, or just the two of us. That was, for me, a really important part of what cemented our friendship. There were no platitudes from him, none of 'Oh, God moves in mysterious ways.' I couldn't have borne that. It was about us seeking comfort and strength. So those were the people that I was communicating with; they'd be at the house, or at the end of the phone.

It was as if I was locked in a small circle of grief. Colin's side of the family – Ken and Wendy and Ian – came together; while my friends and relatives supported me and the children, and Josh and Henry. It was very tough for those two: being older, they understood what Colin's loss meant in a way that the little ones had yet to grasp. There was a lot of pain, and anger too, as they mourned the man who'd played such a big part in their lives. And while Ken and I did see each other, we were both so shell-shocked that we had to draw comfort from other sources in that raw early stage. We were too lost to find each other – at first.

Sometimes, I just couldn't believe that this was my new reality. But for the children's sake, I did my best to function as normally as possible, and the day-to-day business of living had to continue.

Tuesday was bin bag day, I remember. We'd lost Colin on a Monday, so of course no one had put the rubbish bags out the next day. But as the next weekly collection approached, I remembered I'd need to go to the garage to collect all the bags from the week before. I braced myself. The garage was Colin's domain: full of tools, boat parts, spare engines.

Suddenly, I could not face going in there alone. My friend Angee was round, checking in on me, so I asked her if she'd come with me.

'Don't I just get all the glamorous jobs?' She squeezed my hand. 'Come on you.'

The two of us filed into the garage. On one side were my first husband's drums, which he had left our son Henry. On the other was all Colin's fishing kit. Nothing had changed: even the smell – dust and diesel oil – was the same. In fact, if I closed my eyes and inhaled that familiar smell, I could almost believe Colin was there standing right in front of me.

Suddenly I began to sob uncontrollably. I felt like a train had just hit me.

'Oh my God, just look at all the stuff. I just can't stand it, Angee I can't stand it. I'm not going to be able to cope. I can't do this!'

Instinctively, almost blinded by tears, I reached up for the shelf where Colin's dinghy engine was kept. 'Oh, Colin, Colin, where the fucking hell are you?' I wailed.

Angee, standing with her arm around me, gave me a hug.

'Er, Jane,' she said gently, 'wrong dead husband!'

Wiping my eyes, I looked up: rather than the shelf full of Colin's stuff, I had my hand on the shelf holding my first husband's drum kit. How I will always love Angee for piercing the sorrow with humour. We laughed and cried together, almost hysterically.

'Oh fucking bollocks and fucking shit,' I shouted at no one, '*I just want Colin back.*'

I needed those moments of release. Another day, my dad was round, Tim from the Mission and a lady called Sylvie from my local church; Stephen, the minister, too. We were trying to sort something out and I was explaining what was causing me a problem – something to do with money or paperwork had been difficult, people weren't listening, I couldn't get through to the right person. Little did I know that that would just be the start of me against bureaucracy.

'It's like banging my head against a bloody wall, I can't get through to these people,' I said, frustrated.

That was when my dad – worried that I might explode – said, 'Oh well, you know, you'd better calm down.'

And that was the trigger: didn't they realise that all I was doing, every bloody hour, was trying to stay calm, keep it together, and he was telling me to calm down? I lost it. It was an explosion: the first and only time I came close to losing control. I just went totally mad.

'Don't fucking tell me to fucking calm down!' I screamed. 'Fucking hell!' I started kicking the door, all the time spewing profanities and screaming at the top of my lungs. 'I hate my fucking life!' It all came out, all the fury and despair and pain I'd been keeping inside, out in this hurricane of words and noise and force. Afterwards I just fell to the floor, sobbing.

My poor dad was saying: 'Oh, steady on, steady on!' He didn't know how to calm me, it was so out of character for me to behave like that, and especially after days of staying really controlled even as events unfolded. I can be fiery, but I don't lose it, not like that. Not ever.

Today, looking back, if someone else told me that story about herself, I would say, 'Well, that's totally understand-able. You were under so much pressure.' And actually, I needed to explode, because I'd contained it all for weeks. But at the time I kept thinking, I don't do this. This is not how – I don't behave like this. This is not what I do. This is not what I do. And, just as I'd felt throughout the whole time since Colin had been missing, there was still a tiny part of me watching and observing: oh, for God's sake, what are you doing?, there was still enough of me that wasn't lost in the maelstrom, that knew that at any moment soon I'd have to pull myself back. However close I came, I couldn't quite lose myself – I maintained a scrap of control.

But goodness me, I needed that release: I let off a lot of steam, and there's nothing like swearing for doing that. And everyone in the room knew it. They were so lovely with me, all of them: a crisis really does sort the wheat from the chaff. Tim, in particular, was just wonderful. 'Oh, that's been a long time coming,' he said. He got on the floor beside me, put his arm round me – just stayed with me. He was so wise.

By this time, I'd got to know more about the stranger who turned up on my doorstep that day. Tim, who's from Wales, lived with his wife and family in Lowestoft, home to our nearest Fishermen's Mission office. He hadn't a fishing or seafaring background. Instead, it was a life of helping people which had led him to that job: he'd worked for 20 years with people with mental health and learning disabilities and, for a spell, with the homeless – always with people who needed support.

I'd also learnt a bit more about what the Mission was all about. It had been founded by a man called Ebenezer J. Mather, who'd visited a North Sea fishing fleet way back in 1881 and been utterly shocked at the conditions the fishermen lived in. 'Let those who speak of the price of fish spend one night aboard a trawling smack,' he once wrote. 'You must be prepared for the grey wilderness of a floating ocean, swept by winds as cold and pitiless as the hand of death!' The language might be a bit flowery, but the sentiment certainly hadn't dated. And old Ebenezer had actually done something about it: setting up what would become this charity to help fishermen and their families in need. At root, the Mission is a Christian organisation, but it supports whomever is in need in a loving way, with non-judgemental kindness: everything you would want from a faith in action. In Tim they'd sent me someone who epitomised all of that: he was a really big bloke, with an even bigger heart.

He ended up spending huge amounts of time down here, even staying in a B&B and being put up by Stephen, our minister, on one occasion. And he'd just help in whatever way he could. For instance, because I didn't drive at the time and didn't have money for taxis, one time he took me to the doctor's surgery, as I had a really nasty chest infection. He sat in the waiting room while I went in, then took me back home again. I couldn't face the looks and murmuring, you see – 'Oh that's Jane Dolby, she's just lost her husband' – I just wanted to get in and out and back home as quickly as I could. So Tim was a great help.

I'll never forget the episode with Coco the kitten, though. This was just a few months into, well, our life after Colin. Amelia had asked for a kitten for her birthday, so the day before Colin died, we'd responded to an advert in the local paper and secretly visited a local lady who had a litter needing homes. Colin had picked out Coco as a surprise birthday present for his daughter, so for Amelia, beyond even a little girl's usual affection for a pet, Coco had huge significance – the very last gift her daddy would ever choose for her.

But at some point on the day in question, Tim left the house to get his laptop from the car and this kitten had gone missing. As we hunted around the house, it became worryingly clear that Coco must have slipped out of the house in those moments when the door was ajar. You can imagine the horror that inspired – as Amelia hunted for her kitten, Tim felt so guilty. We were literally on our hands and knees looking up and down the road, all the time calling, 'Coco! Coco!' Of course, we eventually found the kitten upstairs, curled up on a bed *inside* a duvet cover, and fast asleep. As for Tim, I've never seen someone look so relieved.

I'm sure he gave a little prayer of thanks that day – as did I.

There was one surprise for me. One day, Tim was on a routine visit to mine when I asked him, 'How many people have you helped in this situation, where they've lost somebody and the body is missing?'

'Actually, you're the first one since I've been with the Mission that I've been involved in,' he said. 'Obviously the Mission has been involved in lots and lots.'

I was quite surprised by that: he'd been so good, so steady, in offering me help. He'd been asking his colleagues for advice and support as well, he explained; they described it as the Fishermen's Mission family – and it was one that had embraced me.

The Worst and Best of People

One day, in those dark winter weeks, a lady called Sandra arrived on the doorstep. I didn't know her well, only because her daughter was in the same school year as Henry, and she knew that I wouldn't want to talk. 'Don't be offended,' she told me, her arms straining under the weight of the heavy bags she was carrying. 'I'm sure Christmas shopping's the last thing on your mind. I've got some stuff for the kids.' And she had bin liners full of presents for them: a skateboard for Liam, I remember, and other lovely gifts.

'Thank you,' I said, quite taken aback. And off she went again, no fuss. It took a few moments for it to sink in. Her husband had a successful business and they'd been generous. But it was the thoughtfulness of what she did that touched me: her thinking, oh, I bet Jane doesn't feel like Christmas shopping – and doing something about it.

Indeed, in the weeks that followed Colin's disappearance, I have never felt so abandoned – but so blessed. I started to experience the most unbelievable support from people in my community: my church, my neighbours. I lost my husband and suddenly I was enveloped in this blanket of love, really – there's no other way of saying it. It brings me to tears to think of it, even now. I received love and kindness from some very unexpected places, from people I didn't even know.

People turned up with food in bags, casseroles. Total strangers were putting supermarket vouchers through our door. One of the mums at Amelia's school held a collection, quietly putting the money through the letterbox. The fishermen all had a collection too. There were a few, in particular, who went beyond the call of duty to help us. The local community of musicians and bands also rallied round, holding a benefit gig in Westcliff one night. I wanted to go, but I just wasn't up to seeing people, facing the inevitable questions: 'How are you doing? Have they found anything yet?' But I was deeply grateful. We were not wanting at all. I wasn't up to phoning people back, engaging in conversation, but I texted everyone I could, telling them: 'I'm sorry, I can't see you at the moment but I want you to know how grateful I am.'

In sum, my community was amazing. In about three weeks the people of Leigh-on-Sea had raised thousands to help me and my family through the aftermath of Colin's loss, knowing – before I did, really – that we'd be in need of more than emotional support. It was just incredible. It felt like so many people were rooting for us, wanting to help. It could be painful: everywhere I went there were pictures plastered up in windows: the front page from the *Echo*, Colin's face cut from the papers. In fact, it got to the point where I had to go to a couple of local shops and say, 'Look, please could you take the pictures down, because we have to walk past those to take the kids to school.' But I knew the intentions were good.

Tim from the Fishermen's Mission sprang into action too, funnelling the money to me and the family as and when we needed it. Nobody had planned this outpouring of support, it was just the way it happened – people would have a collection and ask: 'How do we get this money to the family?' And he'd say, 'We're administering it,' so they'd give it to the Mission to look after and distribute. At one point, the Mission actually kept the roof over my head. Water was pouring in because of the tiles the wind blew off our roof that day Colin was lost and I had no money to pay for anyone to fix it. It was expensive, too, because there was a lot of damage. The Mission sorted that out.

In fact, I knew that we could have lost everything – even ended up homeless – had it not been for the people who helped us. One day I will repay them, I promised myself. I will repay them and say 'thank you' – properly. It really was unprecedented, the kindness. I mean, people are unbelievable. As awful as people can be, there are beautiful, incredibly generous people in the world.

It was an eye-opening time, too: the pretences were stripped away as I saw what people were made of. I was astonished that a few who I really assumed would be in touch didn't contact me at all, didn't send so much as a text message. Realising that some friendships and relationships I'd treasured were fair-weathered was a real shock. I had to fight hard not to feel bitter and resentful towards people I felt had let me down. The thing is, grief makes you feel isolated even when people are surrounding you, so you're so sensitive to any hurt. And a death can make people behave oddly. Just seven days after Colin's death, it had been Amelia's eighth birthday. Her party was already booked so, just as I'd stuck to our swimming plans, I went ahead with it. She'd lost so much already, how would it benefit anyone to miss her party too? But even though I hid it from Amelia, it stuck in my throat that only one mother offered to help me run the party along with my brother Robin and my sister-in-law Siobhan.

Today that anger has gone: I know that people often do nothing because they think they don't know how to approach someone who's been bereaved; they worry they are intruding. And I understand how not wanting to do the 'wrong' thing can result in a sort of paralysis. But I will never forget the playground mums who in those months of suffering noticed my pain and exhaustion and invited my kids to tea, or over to their houses at the weekend. It takes an awful lot of energy every day to paint a smile on your face for your children when your heart is breaking. I don't think these women will ever know how much they helped me.

But I had to laugh at some of the ways people responded to the news that my husband had died. About three weeks after we had lost Colin, the milkman knocked on our door.

'Morning, love,' he said chirpily, 'your old man's body been washed up yet?'

'Er, no,' I said, stunned. 'No news yet.'

'Oh, what a shame, love,' he replied. He paused for a

moment and looked up from his clipboard. 'That'll be £8.22, darlin', and do you still want as much silver top now?'

Somehow, I stumbled out a response that wasn't, 'Do you know where you can stick your poxy silver top?'

On another occasion I was at the hardware shop a few roads away to pick up a few things, when the chap behind the counter started looking at me beadily.

'Are you the woman whose husband's drowned and you've got all those kids and no one can find his body?'

'Yes, unfortunately,' I said.

'Oh. Well, I know just how you feel.'

'Oh God, it's just terrible isn't it?' He must have lost a loved one too, poor man. 'Unless someone has been on this journey they could never understand how difficult it is. I'm so sorry for your loss.'

'Yeah,' he nodded, 'I know exactly what you're talking about. My dog's been dead three and a half years now and I'll never get over it.'

I'm afraid on that occasion I struggled to maintain my sympathetic expression.

Your dog! I thought. Your bloody dog? How the hell can that compare to the loss of a husband and father? How can you possibly think you understand how I feel?

I didn't say that, though. I just got out of there as quickly as I could.

In time, I was able to laugh at these situations – to see the absurdity. I try to remember, too, that in their efforts to empathise people can only share the worst that has happened to them. And if the worst that has happened is their dog dying, then that's their only point of comparison. Still, while no one was deliberately being unkind or thoughtless, I did sometimes think their comments could be handily collected into a book called *The Worst Things to Say to the Widowed* – and published for the public's general education!

If you're ever in a position where someone you know – or even don't know all that well – has suffered a similar blow, my advice is to ignore your fears and follow your instincts. When you've lost someone you love so dearly and nothing in your world is as you knew it, you're just too broken and too exhausted to reach for help. You need people to reach out to you. Even offers of 'If there's anything I can do' may be well intentioned, but are next to useless, because they put the onus on the bereaved person to decide what it is that they want and then ask for it. You see, you can't ask when you don't really know what to ask for. You need people to take the initiative – and do something practical.

When you are as lost as I was, you need others to find you.

Saying Goodbye

I experienced the one and only physical symptom of my grief on the day of Colin's memorial service. That morning, I suddenly found I couldn't do my buttons up because I was shaking so much, really shaking. 'Sarah,' I said, 'you'll have to do it for me.' Once, as my bridesmaid, she'd helped me get ready for my wedding. Today she was helping me get ready to say goodbye to my husband.

It was a memorial service, rather than a funeral, as we had no body, but I didn't want that to stop us from marking his loss. By then, past Christmas, I didn't think that we would ever find Colin's body – and I was painfully aware that it was such an abnormal situation for the children. When somebody dies, you'd usually be able to bury the body after a couple of weeks, and it was important for me to keep things as 'normal' as possible for the kids; I wanted them to be able to say they'd had a service for their father.

'This is like a funeral for Daddy,' I explained to Amelia and Liam as the day approached.

'Oh, where are we going to bury him then?' asked Amelia.

'Well, we can't bury him or cremate him because we haven't got his body – he's in the sea,' I said. 'But wherever you go in the world, if you're near the sea, you're near Dad.'

I hoped that would reassure them, and I found a lot of peace thinking that as well: that Colin was there, and in a strange way, where he'd want to be. He loved the sea.

The memorial service was held at Leigh Road Baptist Church, in a beautiful joint service with Southend Vineyard, performed by the man who had married us, Steve. He had since moved on from the Vineyard to a church in Leicester, but came back to conduct the service for Colin. Without a car, I had struggled to get to my usual church, the Vineyard, once I'd moved into my little fisherman's cottage, so I had started going to Leigh Road, the local church. Still, Colin, when he didn't work on Sundays, had sometimes driven me over to the Vineyard and quite liked it, because loads of our musician friends went. So I was very much part of both congregations and both communities joined together to support our family.

I asked people not to wear black – I didn't want it to unsettle the children, for them to be confronted by a church full of people dressed in gloom. Everything was for them; it wasn't for anybody else. So Amelia wore a pretty pink dress, and Liam a flowery maroon shirt. That was a little nod to Colin, and his love of loud Hawaiian prints. They both looked lovely.

When I gazed around the church, it was packed, the pews filled, people standing at the back: there must have been three or four hundred people there. I walked down the aisle with the children – and it wasn't Colin waiting for me at the end this time.

But it was a really fantastic service. Set up at the front of the church was a slideshow of photos of Colin, set to 'Every December Sky' by Beth Nielsen Chapman. It was a beautiful song that we'd both loved, which speaks of finding hope even within despair.

Steve told the congregation about his own role in our lives – 'I married Jane and Colin' – and talked about the messages he had shared at our wedding: about love, and marriage, and the ties that bind us. It was very emotional.

Tim spoke, too, about the fishing industry and the world that Colin belonged to. There was one thing that I'd asked him to mention, as I knew that there'd be many fishermen in the pews that day. Through Tim, I wanted to urge them to wear a life jacket at sea, so that if, God forbid, we lost any more fishermen, other women would not have to go through the pain of having no body to lay to rest. The harsh truth is, you see, that a flotation jacket may not save your life if you're in the water for hours and suffer hypothermia, but it should keep your body afloat until it was found.

I didn't speak. I couldn't have. I stayed at the front with the children, and I was careful to take my cues from them. They weren't miserable. That memorial service was difficult, of course, but afterwards my friend Lisa opened her house for everyone and the atmosphere shifted. 'Look,' she'd said before the service, 'have the wake at my house, so you don't have to worry. Just tell me how many people are coming and I'll do everything for you.' So she liaised with the Vineyard, who helped put on a fantastic spread, and everyone went back to hers. It wasn't an unhappy event at all, it really wasn't. It was a proper party, with music, and drinks, and good food. And I'd asked the mums of the children's friends, the little girl and boy whom we'd taken on our last family holiday together to Weymouth, if the two of them wanted to come. After all, they'd been at our house a lot and had known Colin too. So there were children present, playing in the garden, and it all went on till quite late. At one point I remember thinking, it's such a shame that Colin's not here, all his mates are here, he'd really like it. Yes, it was sad at times, and I got tearful at times, and other people got tearful. But it wasn't depressing; it was a proper send-off for our friend, father and husband.

Afterwards, I was glad I'd done it, for Amelia and Liam in particular. I just wanted to normalise, somehow, in whatever ways I could, what was a very abnormal situation. I was utterly focused on the outcome we needed as a family: emotionally stable children who were learning to cope with and manage their pain. So that whole day was for them. And I definitely did the right thing. I admit, I didn't care then – I just wasn't in a state where it was a comfort to me – if we'd had a service or not. But, in a roundabout way, it did help me, for that focus on the children was giving me a reason to keep going.

Sometimes I would be overcome by sadness, not just for their loss, but for their loss at such at young age. As they grew up, would they have more than snapshot memories of him? When I thought of how great Colin's love was for his children, it could almost break my heart. But then I would stop myself. His love and devotion to them is woven into the fabric of who they are and will shape the people they become, I'd tell myself. Even if, one day, they may forget the sound of Colin's voice, his blood is coursing through their veins and his love is imprinted on their souls.

And they reminded me so much of Colin; it was his eyes, his smile – and his humour and love shone through them. Even then, as a very small boy, Liam was already so much his father's son: easy-going, ready to laugh – yet also terribly sensitive and very affectionate. Barely out of the toddler stage, if he felt I needed it, he'd bring me a tissue or say, 'You look a bit tired, Mummy, do you need a cuddle?' One evening, not so many months after we lost Colin, I was sitting with Liam as he was having his dinner in front of the telly – we wouldn't normally have done that, but this particular night we did – and Liam hadn't a drink in front of him. So I kept checking with him: 'Don't you want a drink, aren't you thirsty?' And in the end he said he *was* thirsty, but he didn't want to ask me to get up again. He was only three.

They are Colin's footprints on the earth, I would tell myself, and while they are here, he is never truly gone.

A New Battle

'I'm sorry, love,' said the woman behind the counter. She couldn't quite look me in the eye. 'But that card's been declined as well.'

'Oh, right.' I stared at the bag of groceries in front me. 'Well, I suppose I'll have to leave it for now then. I'll come back later, if you don't mind . . .'

'No problem at all!' She must have been relieved I wasn't about to make a scene.

I held it together until I got outside the shop. Then I couldn't help but let a few tears fall.

In the aftermath of Colin's death, I hadn't had a lot of the worries that might run through the minds of other women in my situation. I never thought, how will I manage, how will I cope bringing up the children? Because I wasn't really thinking about any of that stuff at the time. I certainly wasn't thinking, what does it mean for the family when there isn't a body? I didn't realise any of what was ahead – and that might have been for the best. I couldn't bear a bigger burden; I was just putting one foot in front of the other as it was.

But events soon opened my eyes to what my loss meant in the wider world. About a fortnight after we lost him,

I started receiving another sort of letter among the condolence cards from friends. These were faceless letters from big companies. Our direct debits were bouncing – electricity, gas, everything, I realised.

Of course, I thought: Colin paid for it all and, without him, there was no money coming into our account. Not only did I have bills to pay, the letters informed me, but I was racking up penalty charges on top of those when the direct debits failed.

What was I to do? Our finances left me no safety net. Because we didn't have much money, we lived on credit cards – we owed thousands. Colin would chip away at our debt in the summer, when the fishing was better, and then we'd have to turn to the credit cards when winter came, because there wouldn't be much money coming in. Fishing really can be a hand-to-mouth existence.

Still, at first it didn't even dawn on me that stopping the letters coming would be an issue. To start with, I would cancel the direct debits that were going out in a dead man's name; and then I would worry about how to settle up – perhaps we'd have to come to some sort of agreement.

I phoned up the electricity company. 'I'm really sorry the bills haven't been paid,' I told them, and explained that my husband had just died. 'Can you help?'

'Send us a death certificate,' came the reply.

'I haven't got one yet,' I said – and that was when the veil was lifted.

Without a body, I didn't have a death certificate. I did some research: as I understood it, the law said that a death certificate cannot be issued without a body. I would need to wait for seven years before I could have a certificate – the period after which the law in this country will accept that someone is gone, if there's been no sign that they've been alive. But without an official proof of death, the company wouldn't do anything.

I went to the bank, my local branch, where they all knew us, intending at least to stop the penalty fees racking up as the direct debits kept bouncing.

'What can I do, now Colin's died?' I asked them. 'I need to freeze these fees, because I'm getting these fees on top of everything else. Can you at least freeze them?' I begged. 'I know I've got to pay you.'

No. Everyone was incredibly sympathetic but there was nothing they could do without a death certificate, they told me. But nor could I cancel the direct debits that were racking up the fees, because they were in Colin's name and the bank wouldn't cancel them without speaking to the account holder. Of course he wasn't there. So they couldn't freeze the charges; they couldn't do anything. Everything kept happening just as normal. Every month the direct debits would go out as if nothing had changed, and every month there'd be a charge each time a direct debit bounced. It was awful.

When I tried to do the same with his other outgoings I was read the same script. I couldn't cancel his mobile phone contract. I couldn't cancel his car insurance. I couldn't cancel anything he was paying for, even if it was completely useless to us now. I phoned up everybody Colin was paying by direct debit, but got absolutely nowhere. I could do nothing, absolutely nothing. Everyone wanted to speak to Colin. I started saving all the cuttings from the press, thinking that would be evidence, but of course it's not, not the kind that they wanted – official documents that would, in terms acceptable to them, draw an end to his life. The public sector wasn't any better. When I tried to claim my widow's pension and change our family's tax credit claim, I couldn't get anywhere with the people at the benefits agency. There was no help coming from that quarter.

I didn't know what to do. I couldn't believe it. My husband's dead, I can't find him, I've got these small children to look after, and I've not only got no income, but I can't prove to anybody he's dead? It was like living in a nightmare. I worried, too, that while most people were lovely, some were talking about me, about how I couldn't jump through the hoops these faceless companies were setting me – 'Oh, no smoke without fire,' that kind of chatter. That hurt.

But the worst thing of all was that I was existing in this total emotional and financial limbo: not knowing what to do, not being able to deal with anything. What happened to Colin had made the manageable completely unmanageable. Of course, any death can have terrible consequences for the family left behind. But my situation was being complicated as a tragedy belonging to an age-old way of life – a man lost at sea – collided with the inflexibility of modern-day corporations.

Tim from the Mission was doing his utmost to help,

applying for emergency grants for us. That got me through the immediate aftermath as the demands for money kept coming in. But I knew that it was a plaster on the wound; I hadn't found an answer to this particular dilemma, not yet.

Soon, the issue raised its head again, in a different form. Like many married people, Colin and I had life insurance, the idea being that if something happens to one of you, the person left behind doesn't have to worry about money: bills are sorted, mortgages are paid off, you can keep the roof over your children's heads. Our policy only promised us what was, relatively, a very meagre amount, because you really struggle to take out insurance for a fisherman. You're actually asked: do you work for the military, on a trawler, or for an airline? They know that these are the dangerous occupations. Plus, Colin didn't have anybody else on the boat with him, which added to the risk factor. We couldn't afford higher payments to get better cover, either: what we did have used to cost him £60 a month. I desperately needed the money that the policy would pay out.

However, when I told the insurance company what had happened, I came up against what was becoming a familiar problem. I couldn't access the money the policy entitled me and my family to, because I couldn't offer the paperwork to prove – in their eyes – that Colin was dead. I was getting frantic. How could I prove that my husband was dead when he'd been lost at sea? It was madness.

Aid came from an unexpected quarter. My love of the online world didn't stop when I lost Colin. But instead of spending hours on forums about music and publicising gigs,

I would dip in and out of a bereavement support group I had found. It was a forum that offered a place for people in my position to share our experiences, our thoughts. Pouring my feelings out in this safe environment where others understood was a lifeline for me. One day, I explained that I kept hitting this wall in trying to sort out our finances; that I was really fighting to see a way through the problem.

Another widow replied. She was a lawyer, she explained. Having heard my story, she suggested I consider something called the 'reasonable evidence test', which she believed had been used by families of the 2004 Asian tsunami victims to cut through the paperwork they faced following the loss of their loved ones in circumstances that, like mine, had left them with no body. That could be my route, she said, to getting all these companies to accept that I was a widow. 'You've got to prove beyond reasonable doubt that your husband couldn't have survived,' she said.

Well, that gave me something to do. I set out to prove Colin couldn't have survived what had happened to him – doing my research online, collecting information about how long it was before cold-water shock set in, what the temperature was that dark November day.

It was not an easy task. Some people are great with paperwork. I'm not one of them. I hate record-keeping, so untangling that mountain of our paperwork was one of the hardest things I've ever done. Not only that, but I couldn't afford professional legal advice so I didn't have any help as I took on the banks, credit card companies, Colin's mobile phone company, the insurance company and the benefits agency. Yet in a strange way, I almost relished it: every day I had a mission, and raging against the authorities (something I've always enjoyed) proved a good distraction from the gaping hole in my life. And then there were the moments when I would catch myself, and really think about what I was doing: having to investigate and prove how my husband had lost his life. It was brutal. But at the same time, it wasn't any worse than the reality I had to live with. Nothing was worse than not having him around.

So I kept gathering my evidence: police records, medical information, mobile phone data, marine accident reports, weather reports and radar readings. Slowly, painstakingly, I built a case which showed that Colin could not have survived the treacherously cold water for more than four minutes, that his phone signal had disappeared at the same moment that his boat radar vanished from the grid at 1.02 p.m. that day; that the disappearance took place at the same time a freak gust of wind had been recorded by the Met Office; that there were no boats or vessels in the vicinity in which he could have sheltered. But it took time to do my research – months and months. It was such a long, frustrating process of spending hours on the phone, being put through to different departments of various organisations with nobody able to help me, before I discovered whom I needed to be speaking to, and how to go about things.

In the meantime, the credit card companies kept making calls to the house phone, my mobile, getting increasingly aggressive. It was dozens of calls a week: at worst, 10 calls a day. Can we speak to Mr Dolby? Why has Mr Dolby not been making his monthly repayments? Each time I would have to explain the situation again: 'My husband is dead, he was a fisherman and he was lost at sea.' Yet without me being able to send them proof of his death, they refused to stop hounding me. Most of the time, I remembered that it wasn't the fault of the people I was dealing with. When I'd phone the bank and some young man would tell me, 'Well, we can't help you because there's no death certificate,' I didn't get angry with the poor schmuck on the phone. He didn't make the rules. What's the point of giving him a mouthful? What purpose would that serve? Of course, there were times when I'd be moved to say, 'Well, I hope you never find yourself in this situation.' I couldn't be nice all the time.

One call, in particular, shocked me. One bank holiday Monday – 4 May 2009, my first wedding anniversary as a widow – the phone rang several times. Each time the voice at the end of the phone demanded to know the answer to the same old question: when would payment be made by Colin? Wearily, I would explain what had happened, run through the script of my personal tragedy. It wouldn't stop them calling, I knew.

Still, one of these calls did stop me in my tracks. It could have been a bank, a credit card company, a collections agency, I couldn't say: they all blended into one. The voice on the end of the line told me, 'I know you claim your husband is dead, Mrs Dolby, but without evidence of his whereabouts, quite honestly he could be living in the Bahamas.'

I was filled with such sadness and frustration. How could this faceless woman suggest such a thing? How could she be so cold and cruel? She wasn't to know it was my anniversary, but her comment would be unnecessary on any day of the week.

From that point on, I was even more determined to see my way through this tangle of heartless bureaucracy. I was like a dog with a bone, refusing to listen to anyone who said no to me. I would not have Colin's memory tarnished by the doubt of others.

Finally, using all the evidence that I had collected, I was able to get an interim death certificate. I don't remember whom I submitted it to – the coroner, I suppose. I still have big blanks in my memory around this time. I wonder if it's the brain protecting itself from the trauma. But I do remember the relief at getting that bit of paper, and what it would mean for my family. I'd cracked it. I could show them some official 'proof' that my husband was dead. I can't lie: the sweet satisfaction of proving everyone wrong was pretty fantastic. More importantly, it meant that I could at last access what Colin had set up to take care of me and the family; and I could negotiate full and final settlements with all the people chasing me.

But it wasn't quite the end of the process, even then. I had to be interviewed by an investigator from the insurance company before they would, finally, release my money – to check I really was legit. People aren't always honest and there'd been a recent, high-profile case of a couple who'd deliberately defrauded their insurance company by pretending one of them had died at sea. So that was the kind of thing the insurers were on the alert for, it seemed to me. Their investigator came to the house and we sat down and ran through all the details of what had happened, much like I had done in the police interview. He was pleasant, but it was very formal. I was quite frightened. You know when you go through Customs and, even if you haven't got anything to declare, you feel guilty? That was how it was for me. Still, I got through it, and the insurance company agreed to pay out on our policy – or, as I saw it, what Colin left us.

Bereaved spouses often receive large insurance payouts, and usually have their mortgagees paid off too. Of course, no amount of money in the world can ease the loss; but poverty on top of that loss is an additional burden to bear. Our insurance was pretty meagre, and most of the money went quickly, to clear the debts arising from the fees levied on our accounts during those months when I couldn't prove Colin had died. The rest I used in a way that I thought Colin would approve of – securing our home for our family.

Still, the financial fallout has left lasting scars. I can't help but wonder: the insurance company must have known all along about the existence of the 'reasonable evidence' process that would finally get me out of that terrible financial limbo. They never told me about it, despite me having wept down the phone to them and pleaded for their help. But how could they not have known? Their whole business is to deal with people in situations like mine.

What's more, I continued to suffer at the hands of those companies. Three years ago someone sold off some of Colin's debt – even though it had been cleared – to a collections agency. These people demanded £11,000 from me. 'But there *is no debt*,' I explained, frustrated, 'I paid it off in 2009.'

It was futile. They refused to listen. They insisted that any agreement I had reached with the original creditor no longer applied. They'd taken on the account and wanted their money. 'It doesn't matter what arrangements you made. It's been sold to us – we've taken over the debt now,' and further action would soon be taken against me unless I paid, they warned me.

Fortunately, I'd kept most of the correspondence from that terrible time and still had the contact details of the credit card company employee who'd dealt with my case. Thank God she still worked there, and intervened to stop this agency pursuing a non-existent debt. It turned out that I wasn't the only one in this situation: apparently, the 'debts' of numerous deceased people had been sold to this collection agency. How would an elderly or less tenacious person cope with this sort of treatment? The collection agency was so aggressive and, perhaps even more dangerous, seemed so authoritative.

I'm not one to dwell on what's gone wrong, though. Strange as it sounds, I can see a silver lining to this whole part of the experience. Although it was so incredibly difficult, having the banks and the authorities to deal with was a really good thing for me. In the months after we lost Colin, people would say, 'Oh you're going to get angry,' as if that was a natural part of the grieving process. But who was I going to get angry with? Colin, for going out that day? The sea, for being the sea? God for – well, you see how I was thinking. I'm quite pragmatic: I always think, well what outcome do I want to achieve? And where was getting angry going to get me? It was just going to deplete me. But I do think that I was presented with a challenge that could become a channel for all my frustrations, a really positive one: a way to turn my grief into action; my fury into tenacity; my utter despair at my situation into a conviction that I was going to resolve at least one small part of it.

Still, I wouldn't ever wish all that for someone else in my situation: when you're at your lowest, it's a terrible thing for your burden to be made heavier in any way. Little did I know then, but my experiences would one day play a part in achieving a change in the law. How? I'll get to that later.

Found

Year zero, you could call those 12 months after losing Colin. Everything had to be relearnt, renegotiated, without him in our lives. I had been right on one count: both our children became very anxious about the idea of going in the sea. Although they were happy to swim in a pool – and I was thankful that I had gone swimming with them in those strange early days – I had been justified in worrying how they felt about the water. It's the sort of thing that grows with you, if you've lost your dad that way. But I didn't want what had been such a source of pleasure and freedom for them – and for their father – to become something dark in their lives, so, one July weekend, eight months after Colin's death, I booked us on a day trip aboard a paddle steamer on the Thames. It was my way of trying to rebuild their confidence on the water. The steamer, the *Waverley*, was like one of the old Mississippi ones, a really beautiful boat with timber decks and towering funnels painted red. My lovely friends agreed that we'd all go out for the day, so there were three or four families. I wanted the children to feel it was an occasion, a treat, with their little friends there.

We set off. As we reached the end of the pier, my mobile

rang. It was Garry, the police liaison officer who'd worked so closely with us over the past months. A body had been washed up on Shoebury beach, he told me. 'We strongly suspect it is Colin,' he said.

Shock crashed over me. Just as the children and I sailed out to sea for the first time since it had all happened, the same stretch of water was bringing Colin home. What I didn't know then, but do now, was that the day had a further significance: it was Sea Sunday, when churches all over the world come together to remember seafarers and pray for them and their families.

I couldn't do anything. We'd set sail so I was unable to get off the steamer, had to act as if everything was normal for the children's sake: I still wanted them to enjoy their day. But I confided in my friend Sue. 'I think they've found Colin's body,' I told her.

And about an hour later Garry phoned. 'It is,' he said. 'It's Colin.'

I was glad I was with all my friends when I had that call. It was strange. I'd felt I was really making progress: just a month earlier I'd even learnt how to drive.

The fishermen, having been very generous with their donations to help me and the children, had presented me with a cheque. What shall I do with this? I'd wondered. Perhaps I should take the children on holiday, give them a break? But then, I thought, the thing that would be most useful for the family would be for me to learn to drive.

So, at the ripe old age of 43, I paid for a five-day intensive course, passed my test, bought my car – a silver

Daewoo – and insured it. I texted Michael Bates, the cockle man who was really the face of the fishermen for me: 'I've passed my driving test, I'll never be able to thank you all enough.' And I drove down by the beach, waving: 'Look, I've done it!' Colin would have been amazed and proud, I was sure. I'm doing all right, I'd thought, I can do this. I can do this.

But I had no idea how I would feel when Colin was actually found. It was as if I had just started to recover and then – I was hit again. You see, his body being washed up made it very grim. There had been something almost romantic – in the real sense of the word – in him being lost at sea, almost poetic, like something you'd read about in a fairy tale.

The reality was brutal and horrible. Because there's no poetry in a body that's been under water for nearly a year. There's nothing romantic about that. I wasn't allowed to see Colin, but I know, because I asked. I had nightmares about it when I read the coroner's report and the description of his body when he was found. Garry, the police liaison officer, gave it to me, warning me – 'Do you want it all?' – and explaining what was in it.

Yes, I said. In a way, I wanted to feel that pain because I felt I was sharing it with Colin. It happened to him; he had to die. I was just reading about it.

Just as when he disappeared, there was a flurry of attention from the media. 'Body on beach confirmed as missing Leigh fisherman,' read the local *Echo*. I put out a quote, as before, wanting to make sure that *our* thoughts on it all were communicated.

'Colin was the love of my life and although I am trying hard to rebuild, I don't think I will ever fully recover from this,' I wrote. 'It is incredibly hard for the whole family, especially the children. They adored their daddy and he revelled in family life and fatherhood. To have his body home means we can have a funeral and say our goodbyes properly and finally begin the delayed grieving process.'

I wanted people to know, too, what it meant for their community. I thought for a moment. 'The Dolby family have been fishing on the River Thames for over 300 years so this is not only the loss of a wonderful man but the end of an era for this hard-working fishing family.'

There was a small comfort to all this. When Colin was found, he still had his locket on, the one I'd given him from Amelia that first Christmas after she was born and he'd just become a father. He was still wearing it. It was cleaned and returned to me, which I was glad of. But the real significance of that July day was that we were finally able to lay Colin to rest, almost nine months after he first went missing.

The funeral took place on the 24th of the month, a clear summer's day. Just as I'd done with the memorial service, I avoided anything that would scare the children. I explained to them that, yes, we had had the memorial, but now that we'd found Dad's body we could have a different sort of service – a 'saying goodbye' funeral.

'But we've already had a funeral,' said Amelia, with that inescapable logic that kids have.

'We had a "remembering Daddy" service, my darling,' I said. 'But now we've got Daddy's body back we can have a proper funeral. And' – I kept trying to lighten the atmosphere – 'Daddy was so special he gets to have two funerals!' So I wasn't sombre about it.

It was held at the crematorium, a much smaller affair than the memorial service in church – really, I only wanted family and very close friends there. The memorial I had done for nobody else but the children, but this was for those who had loved Colin.

His dad Ken, I knew, had struggled with the idea of a memorial service. He'd said to me, 'You have one of those *after* somebody's had a funeral.'

And I had had to explain to him why I was doing it. 'It's for the children, Ken. They need it.'

He totally understood, but I knew it had been hard for him. And there'd been loads of people at the memorial, too, and the Dolbys were a quiet fishing family. So the funeral was for them. Still, there must have been about a hundred people there – lots of people from the fishing community came. We'd sung the hymn 'Eternal Father' at our wedding, and we did for Colin's funeral too. Afterwards, we gathered in a local restaurant.

Still, that whole day had a very different feel to the memorial service and the party we'd had at his wake. I didn't expect it to be different – a lot of the faces were the same, Tim Jenkins spoke again – but it was Colin in that coffin. And you know when you go to a funeral and the curtain goes round, and the coffin disappears from sight? When that happened I just couldn't stop crying. I hadn't cried, really, at the memorial service: I'd felt moved, and I'd felt emotional, but it hadn't been proper crying. But I could not hold it in when I saw that. Siobhan, my sister-in-law, was standing behind me and put her arms round me, and I leant my head on her and wept.

Yes, it was very different – because this time, I was really saying goodbye.

The Dark Before the Dawn

Sometimes, in the weeks after the discovery, I would come across press coverage online. It's an odd feeling, to see your personal tragedy made public, however much time passes. The comments below the articles online were sympathetic, of course, and there was often a sense that the recovery of Colin's body would offer us some resolution. 'At least the family can have a funeral and closure, they can start to move on,' read one. 'So, so sad,' read another, 'but at least the family can now try to look forward.' That was my hope, too. But one, I remember, struck a different note: 'This must be like having to grieve twice over.'

And I tried – I kept trying – to move on, but the strength of the blow took me by surprise. Dead but alive, that's all I can describe my state as: a heaviness of the soul. I felt like I was walking around with a stone in my chest, this big, heavy stone instead of a heart – it was the worst I'd felt so far. It brought me low, physically: I could not straighten my back. I ached and was constantly shaky and scared. I desperately wanted someone, anyone, to come and be strong for me and tell me what needed to be done.

I could barely believe that, just a few weeks before, I'd been thinking, this is going to be okay, I can do this, it's hard but I'm going to be all right. I thought I was holding it together, recovering. And I had been all right, for a while, with my painted-on 'Yes, we're managing fine' smile. Suddenly, now, I was thrust into this state that was beyond pain. Months after I had lost Colin, I had to start all over again – and this time it was much, much worse. Any lingering trace of numbness, that feeling of being in a dream state, had dissipated: I finally grasped that this was my new reality.

I hadn't known it would be like this – because I didn't know what shock was. I thought it was an exaggerated version of surprise. I didn't know that it was nature's way of anaesthetising you so you didn't have to face all that pain at once, because you'd go down and never get up again. I didn't realise that it could last for around a year; that as it gradually wears off, it often means that the second year after your loss is harder.

In the grip of despair I found myself behaving in ways I'd never have expected, as I tried to ease the pain. One of the first places I drove to after passing my test was down to Two Tree Island, where Colin had taken me that first time we'd gone out together on his boat. I saw it like this: some people like to peel off a plaster gradually, but I'm all for yanking it off as fast as possible.

I had driven here just once before, during a driving lesson. Concentrating on learning to drive, in the company of my instructor, I was able to keep it together. But when I drove here alone it was a very different story. I could picture Colin just as he'd been that first night, sitting beside me – holding my glance just that beat too long for us to be 'just friends'.

'I've never been down here at night, it looks completely different,' I said.

'Don't worry, love' – Colin gave me a reassuring wink – 'I know this road like the back of my hand, I could drive down here with my eyes closed.'

I smiled back at him.

It was too much. As the memories overwhelmed me, the tears started to flow. I felt so close to Colin, but it was so very wrong to be there, alive in his world, with him no longer a part of it.

I put my foot down and drove faster – much too fast, probably, along those winding lanes and over the humps in the road. Every time I went over one too quickly and got that unsettled feeling in my stomach, it was a split second of respite from the endless pain. But it wasn't enough. With my windows up, I started screaming at the top of my lungs, tears rolling down my face. I was absolutely desperate to empty myself of the intense grief I contained all day, every day. I must have looked like a madwoman to anyone who saw me, but I didn't care. Somehow, shouting with all my might seemed a way to release these huge emotions. And I think it did help, just a tiny bit – but it was like shovelling coal with a teaspoon. My burden was too much.

Unable to escape my grief, I searched for answers as to why it had happened – and how. I longed to know every detail of Colin's last moments. I think it may have been the only way I felt I could join him in his suffering. By reliving it, perhaps I thought I could share that burden with him. So I went over and over the facts I had, drip-fed by updates from the police and the authorities.

Slowly, a picture was emerging of what exactly had taken place that November afternoon. Colin's body had been found in the same area where his boat had gone down: he'd been washed ashore on the bit of beach directly parallel to where the *Louisa* was found. Had he, I wondered in the days after Garry broke the news, been trapped underneath something on the seabed, before at last becoming dislodged? It seemed so very unlikely that, after all those months, he would have just drifted on the currents back round to that exact point.

But I couldn't get an answer – not really. The authorities did have some marine investigators trying to work out what had happened to the boat. Their report, based on the examination of the boat, concluded that the storm sank it – through the sheer force of the waves.

Ken, I knew, thought differently. We'd talk it over, when we could face broaching the subject.

'That boat was designed to go through a storm,' he told me, 'it would only have gone over if it was sideways onto a wave.' What's more, Colin had apparently been saying he'd had trouble with the engine. I would chew over these facts in my mind. If the engine had cut out – for whatever reason – the boat could have swung sideways, putting him in a terribly dangerous position. So was Colin perhaps down in the engine room trying to sort the engine out when the boat overturned?

In the end, we could only speculate – and that wasn't what the report said. But I do trust Ken's judgement: he's so experienced and knowledgeable. He only stopped going out fishing with Colin a few years before he died, and Colin himself used to say he still learnt so much from his dad, from all that experience.

There were other lingering questions. Colin was pretty much alone on the water that day, I was told – and I'm still not clear why there weren't other fishermen out. I don't know if a storm was forecast and, though it was calm in the morning, they thought, 'We'd better not.'

Once, I dug out a newspaper weather forecast for that day: 'Cloudy with outbreaks of rain, heavy at times. Strong south-westerly winds with a risk of gales in the south-east.'

I don't know whether Colin had looked at the sea and thought, 'Well, it's going to be a short day, I'll be back before the storm.' I don't know what he was thinking.

What ran through my mind, however, was that we were broke, and that it was nearly Christmas. That time of year is the quieter period for fishermen, and we'd got Henry, Amelia and Liam all with birthdays close together in the run-up to the festive season, then Christmas Day itself, my brother's, my niece's birthdays too: lots of family celebrations in the space of just a few weeks. Was the lack of money driving him? Did Colin feel under extra pressure to provide for us all? I'll never know. But I do know he was doing what he always did: going out to sea to look after his loved ones.

What was harder to bear was that I would never know

how he died. I didn't know what had happened to him. He could have been knocked unconscious – that's what I told the children, to reassure them: 'Chances are he was knocked unconscious before he hit the water.' And he might have been knocked unconscious. But after he was found, it triggered something in me. I tortured myself with what else he might have gone through – the agony of drowning – going over and over and over it in my head. Was he scared? Had he hurt himself? Was it hypothermia that killed him, as the water was so bitterly cold? Or did he drown? What did it feel like to gasp for air yet have water fill your lungs? How aware was he of what was happening? Perhaps he banged his head and – please God – knew nothing?

It stopped me sleeping. I'd wake up at night with my heart pounding, gasping for breath, thinking about what it was like for him. My head would be filled with scenes of him falling into the water, his panic increasing as he plunged deeper, the surface light moving further away. Sometimes it was as if I was seeing things through Colin's eyes: I'd be sinking, the water surrounding me getting darker. There were times when I could have hit my head against the wall to stop the thoughts coming; I had so little control of what I was imagining. I was reliving those moments a thousand times a day. Even today I have to remind myself that whatever he went through, he only had to suffer it once – stop myself endlessly replaying events in my mind.

I couldn't face my life as it had become. The desolation, the loneliness, the despair and the sheer, crushing, bloody hopelessness of it all were indescribable. I wanted to spend hours looking at photos of Colin or watching little video clips, where I could still hear his voice, or just see him move. I had a powerful urge to walk and walk, to search for him, even though I knew I'd never find him again. My head knew that, but my heart didn't. I longed and pined for him constantly. I began to understand why the Middle Eastern widows we see on TV news wail and beat their breasts – it's all I wanted to do, too. I needed some tangible manifestation of my anguish, so people would know the world was no longer the same.

I developed an overpowering need to tell people, often strangers, my story – which must have been desperately embarrassing for them. And it wasn't that I didn't care, but the normal rules of day-to-day life no longer applied. I just needed to hear myself say, 'My husband has died.' Perhaps, instinctively, I hoped that saying the words would resonate internally; that they would help me accept that Colin was really gone.

Yes, time was passing, but it certainly wasn't getting any easier. Colin missed Liam's first day at school, that first September after we lost him. I did that alone – it was horrible. I wasn't the only mum on her own as the family photos were taken, but I couldn't even tell my husband about it later, show him the photo or anything. I went home and sobbed and sobbed, thinking of what Colin had missed, what he'd been robbed of.

And I didn't recognise who I was. I became this version of myself that I didn't like: irritable with the children, needing all my energy just to function. At the slightest thing that demanded any more of me, I would snap, 'Oh, for goodness' sake, what is it now?' And I was *never* like that with the kids. I became irritable with other people, too, unsympathetic and intolerant of any complaints. If a friend said a throwaway thing like, 'Oh, we can't have a holiday this year,' I'd think to myself: 'Well at least your husband's still alive' – with such venom.

That's not me! But I just lost myself for a while. Everything I did was underpinned by sorrow, this deep, deep sorrow, which manifested itself in a lack of patience and intolerance. I felt stuck. I used to say to those I was closest to, my good friends and family: 'I don't like who I am and I don't know how to return to who I was.' I knew, you see, that I couldn't go back – I was never going to go back to who I was again.

To my surprise, I found I couldn't even sing any more – even in that casual, absent-minded way we sing along to favourite songs when we hear them on the radio. I used to get a terrible lump in my throat, get choked. Actually letting my voice out was impossible. Whenever I tried, I was unable to contain my emotion and, within a few notes, was reduced to sobbing. I think I had buried so much of my pain to keep functioning for the children, but singing somehow tapped into my true sorrow – and released agony and grief from the very core of me. It was as if I could keep a hold on everything and carry on, but if I tried to sing the walls would come tumbling down.

So I simply stopped doing it. Singing is something I used to do, I told myself. I need to get on with looking after the children, trying to be mum and dad and keeping a roof over our heads. Who cared, nowadays, if I never sang again? Not me, not the kids, not Colin – not anyone. It just didn't matter enough to me – not any more – to pursue a solution, even if there was one. I had more pressing priorities than whether or not I could harmonise along to the radio. So, in the months – and indeed years – that followed, I was silenced.

I still turned to music, but in a different way: when I had a moment alone I'd put on my headphones, turn up the volume as far as it could go and just lie on my bed, letting the tears come. I wanted to blast every terrible thought out of my head – and the best way I knew of doing that was to fill it with the loudest music.

There was just one thing I clung to. My elderly aunt Joyce had been widowed a few months before me. A couple of months into my own journey, she took my hand and said, 'Jane, I want you to know, it gets worse before it gets better.' At the time I had listened and nodded. How could it get worse? But when her prediction became my daily reality, I would try to hold onto her words. 'It's part of the process,' I would tell myself. 'As much as I feel like I'm heading for the loony bin, I'm not going mad.' Later, I would learn that my experience – hitting this trough about a year after I lost Colin – was not uncommon. If you hang out in the 'hood' – the widowhood – this delayed reaction is known as the 12-month low. It's the reason that many bereavement counsellors often advise people to wait until a year after their loss before they begin counselling. I didn't think it at the time, but they were right.

Little did I know then that from rock bottom there would be only one path ahead of me: upwards.

New Beginnings

I couldn't go on as I was doing, I knew. I had to find a new way of life, a different way of living – without Colin. But what? I couldn't see a future for me. Everything had changed, every part of the life that I'd built for myself had been shattered and undermined.

As a single mum once again, I knew I had to work. In recent years I'd had my hands full with the kids, but before that I'd had this life of going to gigs, trying to help bands and singers, writing press releases about them, trying to drum up a bit of a buzz. But now, who gave a flying fig if somebody got a record deal or not? After struggling with what I'd been through, not having any money except what people gave us, months of not being able to access any help as a widow, I certainly didn't – not any more. I had totally lost interest in anything to do with music. The joy had just gone out of it for me. It seemed like such an empty, meaningless, vacuous world.

No wonder that I wasn't at all sure what my next step would be. The answer came in the form of my friend Lisa, who had hosted Colin's wake at her house. She's a glamourpuss with an hourglass figure and long blonde hair – but what you can't see at a glance is the size of her heart. I'd met her at Southend Vineyard church years earlier, and she'd been such a rock to me. Lisa told me that the charity she worked at, Southend YMCA, where she ran volunteering activities, needed a press officer. The job involved working with disadvantaged young people, she said, and would be a good fit with my experience in dealing with the media in the days when I used to do promotion.

I wasn't convinced. I've got enough disadvantaged young people of my own, I thought. Why on earth would I want to go and work in a place where I'll be surrounded by even more of them? But I was desperate for some money. I'd lived on what had been given to me and it was running out. I had to get work and knew I wasn't in a position to be choosy. I applied for the job, and got it.

So, about a year after Colin's death, I started work as a press officer at Southend YMCA for an initial period of three months – around 24 hours a week to begin with, when the kids were at school. My first task was to help a couple of young people set up and publicise a group for looked-after children. It was an absolute revelation. Suddenly I was involved with this organisation that was working with the most vulnerable, disadvantaged children and young people in the area. They all had their own story. You might hear that this boy's sole parent had died and he'd gone into care; or that this girl had a lovely background but suffered terrible bullying at school. Some of the kids had experienced abuse, domestic violence, bereavement; they had parents who were grappling with unemployment, poverty, mental health problems or addictions – it was the full gamut of things that can go wrong for children.

Without trivialising my family's experience, working there helped me to see things from a different perspective. There's more than one kind of suffering, I realised. I started to understand that I'm not the only person shitty things have happened to. And somehow, what I had been through would help me to help somebody else. I just absolutely, with all my heart, felt I was meant to be there; that I was doing something that mattered.

And that was the start of things getting better for me. Working with those wonderful young people and being in that environment was exactly right for me. Even if I won the Lotto, I'd still want to work there. And, on a lighter note, as with any role, I was meeting new people, getting out of the house, having to put a professional head on – it made me feel better. We did have a real laugh in the office, too. Lisa was my manager, but she was my friend first, and our working relationship was just fantastic. We became like sisters, really. We're still very close now. Slowly that heaviness I was carrying, that deadness inside, started to lift. The pain that had been driving me to snap at the people I was closest to was beginning to ease. I began to look forward to going to work – even, sometimes, feeling something of a spring in my step. My friends must have been very patient with me through that process, that metamorphosis. And I was very, very glad when, with the passage of time and this new avenue in front of me, I started coming through it.

It wasn't easy. I wasn't myself for a long time, probably

much longer than I thought when I was going through it – maybe two, three years. I had such trouble letting Colin go. Everything was so much effort, simply because I was carrying such a load of pain. Some days, too many days, I still felt as if I couldn't even breathe, that I had a great big stone in my throat. I'd feel separate from the world, in a bubble, that everyone else was busy doing all this – stuff – and I wasn't really part of it. I would even catch myself, at moments, listening to myself speak, I was so detached, just going through the motions. It took me some time to realise that my pain, separating me from the world, was a way of remaining connected to him. And it wasn't that I woke up one day and thought, right, I'm not going to feel this way any more. But eventually I came to realise something. If there were such a thing as ghosts, or an afterlife, Colin wouldn't be able to get there, because I was holding onto him so tightly.

Two things helped me. When I was in that terrible place, I desperately needed hope that I would be okay – if not soon, eventually. I found that hope in my widows' group, which I'd come across online and stayed a part of. It truly was a lifeline, as I'd speak to women in my position but six months, or a year, or two years, further down the path of widowhood, and hear that, yes, it could get better. Many were becoming true friends, whom I'd met up with in 'real' life. About six months after I lost Colin, we'd even gone on a short trip to York with our kids. I was still so raw that it was far from fun and games for me, obviously. But it had just helped me to be part of something. For me, there's a great comfort in people. Some people lock themselves away, withdraw from the world, when they are low and vulnerable, but I have an overwhelming need to connect with the world when I'm at my lowest. That's just who I am.

And I had my faith. I had never leant so heavily on God before. I wasn't someone who'd go to church regularly – though there'd be spates when I did – but I don't think you need to go to church to have a faith. I've found fellowship in other ways: many of my friends are Christians and I'd think nothing of phoning Lisa and saying, 'Can we pray together?' And then I'd pray, yes, out loud. I'm not shy! I might pray to the Holy Spirit to intervene in a situation, to give me wisdom, to give me guidance. It's so much a part of my life that I don't have to rock up on a Sunday; I feel like I'm in a permanent relationship with God. So I really clung to those two aspects of my life.

Still, even when I was on this path of recovery, something remained changed, deep inside me. I don't think I'll ever get back to the version of myself that existed before Colin died. Always a worrier, I'd become so much more anxious about things, even a bit of a catastrophist. When you've had bad things happen, they become part of your DNA. Your default position is: what's the worst that can happen? Because it probably will. And I'd struggle to reassure myself that it wouldn't, because I knew from experience that it could. The biggest fear I lived with – still live with – was about something happening to me: if I were gone too, what would happen to the children? Being an only parent is totally different to being a single parent, a completely different level of responsibility, I was finding. However irritating your ex may be, it does normally mean that there's someone else who loves the kids as much as you do – as well as the occasional weekend off. I'd be gripped by fear just thinking about the possibilities. I had to work quite hard to reassure myself that just because something terrible had happened, it didn't mean that something terrible would happen again.

And I wanted to choose not to live in the past or be the miseryguts at a perpetual pity party. I deliberately made a point of not turning everything into an anniversary to mark in the years to come. Today, I couldn't tell you on what date we held the memorial service, in those months after Colin's death. I know that's astonishing, given its significance, but I didn't want the calendar to become filled with dates with a shadow over them. Of course, some were etched in my memory. Colin's birthday, the day I lost him.

And every so often, slowly but surely, another of the big life events would arrive – and Colin would not be there. As the year 2012 rolled round, with all the hullabaloo and celebration that marked the London Olympics, I was painfully aware that he had so looked forward to sharing this time with his son. In the event, Liam – as a child born on 20/12, in the year the Games were announced – was there for the opening ceremony and for a little boy who loves sport it meant so much. We also had two tickets, front row for the Paralympics, and my brother Robin, the most incredible uncle to my kids, took Liam to watch the competitors. Of course, his dad was supposed to have taken him. But he couldn't.

Amelia's 13th birthday was another such milestone; and I still find every Christmas extremely difficult. At all these events, which are so family-oriented, there is always a reminder that I am not quite like other people. It's that relentless need to dig deep, to do everything, to make it all okay, to smile – it takes quite a lot of energy. Sometimes I feel as if I try so hard to make other people feel special, yet I am no longer special to anyone.

Aside from our loss, we were still dealing with the aftermath of the death on a practical level. Money was extremely tight, now that Colin was gone, even with me earning at Southend YMCA. It got to the point where I had to pawn Amelia's locket – the one that Colin had brought back to me – and our wedding rings. I stood in that pawnbroker's sobbing as I handed them over, but I was so broke I had no choice. But I bought it back at the first opportunity I got: I kept paying the interest to stop them selling the locket and as soon as I'd saved enough money I went straight back in there to buy it. I didn't see it as an extravagance: it was absolutely the right thing to do. I'll get our rings back too, in time.

There was something else I saved up some cash for at about that time. I took a step towards tackling the block on singing that had dogged me through the years. I found a local vocal teacher, a chap called David, whom I clicked with when I spoke to him on the phone. I just liked his style: he was less about hitting the 'right' notes and more about helping students find their voice and build confidence. In person, he was patient and encouraging.

'What's your favourite song?' he asked me – and then I simply sang along, my voice increasing in volume along with my confidence. I was so relieved that I could do it – no tears, no lump in my throat. Somehow, being led through the process by a professional had helped me to divorce the experience of singing from my personal grief.

I only went to see him a couple of times as I couldn't afford more, but taking the decision to sing was a turning point for me. From that moment onwards I was able to sing along to the radio, to a CD, without being overcome by tears.

Music wasn't back in my life yet, not really, not in any significant way, but it was a start. That was a blessing – and a blessing, as I would soon find, that would continue to multiply.

A Chance to Give Back

It was in the spring of 2012 – 14 years after I'd first gone out on Colin's boat – that I started thinking about the promise I'd made in my darkest hour: to repay the help the Fishermen's Mission had given me. I can do something for the Mission, I thought. I feel right now; I can give back.

How I'd go about it was the puzzle. I wasn't a sponsored walk, or run, or climb sort of woman. And there was no way on God's sweet earth that I'd ever manage a sponsored diet, no matter how much I thought I should lose a bit of weight. What I did know about was music, I mused.

Then it came to me. Just that last Christmas, I'd watched the Military Wives Choir have a number one hit with their song 'Wherever You Are'. The singing group had been created for the BBC programme *The Choir*, made up of the wives and girlfriends of men serving in Afghanistan, and they'd gone on to have considerable chart success. My ambitions were much smaller, but I thought: why can't we have a maritime version – the Fishwives Choir? I'd ask a couple of the girls married to local fishermen if they'd like to record a karaoke-style CD, then we could sell a few in the pub and, I hoped, raise a couple of hundred quid for the Mission and get the cause a bit of attention.

So, on the morning of 17 April I created the Fishwives Choir page on Facebook. 'Who'd like to participate in a recording to fundraise for the Fishermen's Mission?' I wrote. 'Send me a message if you'd like to join the Fishwives Choir.' I 'tagged' a few of the women I knew locally who were married to fishermen; Colin's sister Wendy; Tim and the Fishermen's Mission; and a couple of other women who were related to fishermen. I hardly knew any potential fishwives really, maybe three or four girls. Then I logged off to get on with my day. Little did I know where that seemingly insignificant little post would lead.

A couple of days later, I logged in again to check my replies. I saw messages from Wendy and a few of the other local women. 'We'd love to get involved,' they told me. 'Where do we start?'

But that wasn't all. There were other names, names I didn't recognise and, when I clicked through to their profiles, I could see they weren't all from Leigh; they were from all over the country. My post about the Fishwives had been public, so people had been able to share it with their friends. 'I heard about the choir,' they told me. 'I saw so-and-so post about it on Facebook,' or 'My friend so-and-so told me about it.' Then they'd explain their own connection to the sea. 'I'm married to a fisherman,' one would tell me. 'I'm the daughter of a fisherman,' another would say, 'my family's always worked the sea.' And, yes, in some cases, 'I'm the widow of a fisherman – like you.' But regardless of their circumstances, they all asked the same question: 'How can we get involved with the choir?'

In the days that followed, the messages kept flooding in. I got into organising mode: I was very official! I had a form people had to fill in if they wanted to get involved, stating their connection to the industry. With my usual tendency to worry, I wanted to be able to document everything if anyone ever asked. But the silver lining to this was that I started learning everyone's personal stories.

There were some familiar faces signing up, among them my friend Wendy – not to be confused with Colin's sister of the same name – who'd sung at my wedding and, in fact, we'd been pregnant together at the same time with our daughters. Slim and dark-haired, she'd made a good career as a professional singer, gigging, singing on adverts. People say music is a hard life – the late nights, the long drives to gigs – but it keeps you youthful, I think, it's the spontaneity of it all. Her fishing connection was through her family in Norfolk: her uncles were eel fishermen. And thank God for that link, I thought – because she had a fabulous voice.

My good friend Lisa, the blonde bombshell, was another. I'd been round at her house one day when I'd idly said to her, 'Oh I wish you had a fishing connection, I'd love you to be involved.' Her parents were there too, and her dad had piped up: 'What about old Donkey Brandon, does that count?' It turned out this relative had apparently been in the industry, moving the fish from the boats and working around Billingsgate fish market – yes, with a herd of donkeys. So she was in, too.

Then there was Lee, whom I'd also known for ages.

We'd had our older boys around the same time and there'd been many an evening when, with our children playing in the garden, we'd sat as dusk fell, candles flickering, singing songs and playing the guitar. Lee was a nurse, but her former partner had set up a company building boats and providing skippers, crew and maintenance technicians to the offshore wind farm business. They'd employed lots of ex-fishermen who had previously earned their living from fishing British waters, before quota cuts had come in. Lee had got to know a lot about the industry and its men; she'd tell me that she'd been struck by how brave, knowledgeable and hard-working they were.

Strangely enough, she'd had her own brush with danger on the sea. In 2007 she had been on a trip to Antarctica on a tourist ship called the MS *Explorer*, which ran into trouble. Lee and her partner were in bed in their cabin when they hit the ice – they knew, she said, that something was wrong even before the alarms started to sound: they felt the impact. Everyone was safely evacuated to lifeboats and picked up by a Norwegian cruise ship. The ship itself was left lying on its side, surrounded by pack ice, before sinking to the depths of the Southern Ocean some time later. In the hours they spent out on the freezing-cold seas in open wooden lifeboats, waiting to be rescued, huddled together in life jackets, there were moments, said Lee, 'when we really didn't know if we would make it. It was such a reminder of nature's power.' Someone really was looking down on her that day.

But what was surprising to me was that there were local

women whose lives had run in parallel to mine for years, whom I was only just getting to know now, through this choir. From Leigh there was Lara, a hairdresser and local mum who spent her spare time working in the family cockle shed down in Old Leigh. She'd heard about what I was up to, got in touch and, when we chatted, we realised that her and Colin's relatives – the earlier generations – had worked alongside each other; Colin had even played snooker with her uncle and eaten her grandmother's cake! She found some old photographs, and Ken was able to recognise her ancestors, 'Oh, that's so-and-so, I remember him,' and the like.

Lara's heritage was pretty impressive: her grandfather Arthur Dench's boat, the *Letitia*, had been one of the famous fleet of 'Little Ships' involved in Dunkirk, when hundreds of fishermen and other non-military craft helped out the massive wartime evacuation, ferrying soldiers from the French beaches onto their warships at huge personal risk. On the journey home, Lara explained, the *Letitia* ended up towing another cockle boat from Leigh, the *Renown*, as it had engine trouble. Suddenly, in the dark of the night, an explosion lit up the sky – a mine had gone off. The *Renown* was lost, but the *Letitia* survived – with those on board realising that men they'd worked alongside for years had been lost in an instant.

Her family didn't cockle any more, but they still had their cockle shed to run. Arthur himself had started up in 1947 trading from a trestle table, on which he sold shellfish in pints and half-pints for a few pennies. It had grown into a thriving seafood business, Estuary Fish Merchants. Their seafront shed was the only one left in Leigh that still sold to the public, and on sunny days the queue would be out of the door – all the shellfish would go in a couple of hours. 'It's hard work,' Lara told me, 'backbreaking, all the gutting fish.'

Yet sometimes she'd hear people walk past and say, 'Ugh, that's disgusting' about the beautiful display of fresh shellfish, the best you can get. People are so divorced from the reality of what they're eating. Lara just laughed at this – I suppose it helped that they'd also have people who really knew their stuff, like Rick Stein, the renowned seafood chef, come by and go into raptures over it all. Lara, too, was absolutely addicted to the cockles they sold. Apparently her mother, who had worked in the cockle shed, ate loads of them when she was pregnant with Lara, which the family suspected might have something to do with it.

It was quite a leap of faith for her to get involved, looking back. Her friends weren't in the fishing industry, and I know there were a few jokey comments about the singing fishwives: 'What, are you going to wear a net on stage?' After all, Lara herself was more of an R&B girl than a fan of choral music – she'd say I sounded like Chaka Khan or Alicia Keys, which I'd brush off, but it was very sweet of her. The moment we met I thought: she's a blast of fresh air, with really good energy.

Similarly, I didn't know Laura before the choir, another local girl who worked as an office manager and had a little boy. Her husband Daniel fished for cockles out of

Leigh-on-Sea and had known Colin, I found out. Laura hadn't, but she'd known of my husband, heard his name mentioned in conversation. It wasn't until I put the message out on Facebook that Laura and I got in contact, she learning about the Mission and what they did for the fishing community. 'Too close to home for us not to support it,' was how she put it.

Neither she nor Daniel were from a fishing background – he was a bit unusual perhaps, for a fisherman: he loved the sea so much that he'd found his own way to it. At school his best friend was from a fishing family so they used to bunk off together and go and unload the catch that had come in that day. From there, he was hooked. 'So he's been on the water since he was about 15, 16,' she said. 'But if my son ever asks, he stayed in school till he was 18!' And it was their love of the water that had brought them together: Laura had been into the sailing club when she was younger, and Daniel had had leisure boats, and that's how they'd got to know each other.

By the time I met her, her husband had stopped fishing – with her pregnant with their little boy, and the quotas and restrictions ever an issue, he'd called it a day. He'd decided he needed to do something that was more reliable and so had started working as the skipper of a charter boat, doing survey work and other things. There was no chance of a life off the waves, though. 'I don't think I'll ever take him off the water, he'll never leave it,' Laura said to me once. 'He's the only person I know who actually loves their job and would get up quite happily at half past two, half past three, to do it.' I was really glad Laura was involved – it meant I was reaching the women connected to the fishermen who had helped me, through their great generosity and support.

What I didn't find out until a bit later was that both Laura and her husband had been out on the seafront in that terrible week when Colin was missing, and we were still hoping to find his body soon. We were all at Wendy's rehearsing, and Tessa Dunlop – who presents the TV programme *Coast* – had come down for the day to talk to us for a radio programme. She was interviewing Laura, me listening with half an ear – 'What's your connection to Colin?' 'Well, my husband knew him' – when it all came out.

Laura and her husband had gone down to Shoebury coastguard station on the cold November day Colin's boat was raised from the seabed, not so far from the shore. There was a group of fishermen who met down there, waiting for news – all hoping that their friend was on board; hoping for a bit of closure, rather than him being lost at sea. Darkness had already fallen as they stood watching from the slipway.

I felt myself going very still as I listened to her tell that story for the first time – because she'd never told me.

Fishing really is a small world, I thought – there are a lot of people who know each other – but it can tend to be the men who make the connections, not the women who love them. So I was glad that already women were coming together and friendships were being built in this way. Thinking about it more, I could see why the idea for the choir had struck such a chord. Fishing is a dangerous job, and people within the community know it: one in 20 will die or be seriously injured at work. There's not many that would go to work so badly paid with odds like that. A friend once put it in a way that really stuck in my mind, that the story of fishing is like an untold war. And, as in war, those left behind tend to be women, and women aren't traditionally heard in maritime history.

This, I hoped, would be a chance for us to have a voice.

From Little Acorns...

I didn't have much time to think about what all these ladies were expecting from me in return: this thing was about to get bigger yet. It all started when a local newspaper reporter, with whom I'm friends on Facebook, saw my Fishwives post. 'Oh, this looks good,' she said. 'We could do a little story on that.' I jumped at the chance, hoping that it would help spread the word. If it goes out in the local paper, we might get a few more girls involved, I thought.

But after her piece appeared, local radio got in touch. Would I do an interview with them, too? I agreed, and it was during our chat on air that the interviewer said: 'Of course, there are fishing families all around the Essex coast, not just Leigh and the Southend area – should they get in touch with you, too?'

You could almost see the light bulb go on in my head!

'If they want to,' I said, 'definitely.'

About the same time, a lady called Jackie contacted me from Hastings.

'I just heard about your story,' she told me over the phone. 'There are quite a few of us here from fishing

190

families and we're really interested in finding out more and maybe getting involved.'

'That's brilliant,' I said, feeling a leap of excitement. 'How many of you are there?'

'At least eight – maybe a few more.'

'Okay, Jackie, I'm so pleased you called. What's your number?' I scrabbled about for a pen but could only find a crayon lurking in my bag. 'I need to organise somewhere we can all meet and have a practice, I suppose. When I know what the next step is and have a rehearsal sorted out I'll call you and keep you posted. Is that okay?'

'That's great, Jane, I'll look forward to hearing from you.'

So that was how the first group of women was recruited from outside my local area! From then on, they were only ever known as the Hastings girls. And Jackie suggested that I go on the local radio there as well, so I did another interview, this time with BBC Sussex, telling my story and explaining what the Fishwives were all about.

Now that my idea was taking flight outside my little patch of the world, my thinking shifted. It's got to be all or nothing, I decided: I should try and get women from fishing regions all over Britain. If we can get everywhere represented, whatever we produce will be more powerful. So I rang BBC Cornwall, knowing that was another area with a rich fishing tradition, and said, 'This is what I've done, are you interested in the story?' And they said yes.

And it just escalated. More press and radio began to pick up on the story, and each time I had a mention somewhere, there would be more women getting in touch about joining the choir. It really was a PR dream. Radio stations would ring up, asking, 'Have you got any girls from our area?'

And instead of saying a flat no, I'd say, 'No – but I'd love some. Can I come on your show?' Then I'd build up yet more traction.

Some days I did as many as five or six interviews, from early morning slots to midnight broadcasts. 'I'd love to be on the show,' I'd tell producers. 'Nine o'clock? No problem.' Then I'd worry afterwards as to how I'd manage the school run and getting into the office. Or I'd keep one ear pricked for the phone as I cooked dinner for the kids, ready to whisk the pan off the hob and dash into the living room with the handset to do a quick interview. Knowing from my experience promoting bands just how important it was to strike while people were interested, I wasn't about to miss a single opportunity.

Yes, it could be bitter-sweet talking about Colin, talking about what we'd lost, but I was so glad to be doing something in his memory, to honour him. I'd much rather be talking about him, the man he was, how he and other fishermen put themselves at risk every day, uncomplaining, to provide for their families, than sweeping it all under the carpet as if our tragedy never was. And there's a special thing that happens when you're doing something authentic; there's a truth to it that gives it power. I'd never really felt that I was a 'proper' PR person, someone I imagined working out of a swanky London agency, swanning around Soho. I'd fallen into doing promotion, really quite by accident, because Colin had very kindly paid for me to record those CDs and I had to shift them. But goodness me, from the response the idea was getting you'd have thought I was handling the hottest new act in the charts. Meanwhile, I was now receiving daily emails and Facebook messages from women connected to fishermen and the commercial fishing industry. And, as more women got involved, I wasn't the only one to uncover a link to another fishwife.

Sue, from Perranporth in Cornwall, had spotted a mention of the choir on the Facebook page for the men's shanty group the Fishermen's Friends – a couple of them had known her husband, Brian, before he died. They were about 40 miles away in Port Isaac and Brian used to fish at Newquay, but fishermen meet up at the fish market, of course, so there's a network. Her daughter Jennie, Brian's stepdaughter, also said she wanted to get involved.

Sue and I had a lot in common. A few years older than me, she was a mum who'd lost her husband too. Like Colin, Brian had grown up fishing from a young age, in Falmouth, where he was born, and had ended up working on a crab and lobster boat, the *Lamorna*. His dad had been in fishing too. When the boats used to get their propellers caught up in ropes – there's always bits of kit floating around the water – he would dive down and cut the ropes away, apparently. Can you imagine, working away under a boat in the cold, murky water? The thought of that sent a bit of a shiver down my spine.

They'd lost Brian on 28 September 2000. The sea had been too rough to go out, so instead he'd gone fishing of a different sort – angling off the rocks in Newquay – and never came back. Fishermen found his body nine days later, off the headland.

'Nobody thinks he was knocked off by a wave, because he knew the sea well – if a big wave was coming, he'd warn me – so it was probably that he slipped,' Sue told me. 'But nobody really knows, because no one was there.'

For that reason the inquest returned an open verdict, but the post-mortem found that Brian had a fractured skull, suggesting that he could well have slipped and knocked his head on the rocks as he fell.

Thankfully, Sue hadn't had to face the same wait as I did to recover her husband's body – though nine days is, of course, more than anyone should have to bear. But again, the Fishermen's Mission stepped in to support her, and she was keen to pay them back. I put her in touch with another of the local women interested in the choir: Hannah, a talented opera singer whose family was steeped in fishing tradition, and who was also from Cornwall. They chatted over the phone, and decided to meet in person for a meal.

And a strange thing happened. After Brian died, his skipper had sold the boat, Sue explained – it was too much for him to handle, a man on his own. 'I showed Hannah a picture of the boat Brian used to work on, and that's when she said, "Oh! That's my brothers' boat."' The two of them realised that the *Lamorna* had been bought by Hannah's brothers, both fishermen themselves. 'We didn't know until we got talking, and that's what made Hannah finally decide to do the Fishwives,' said Sue. 'It was like fate brought us together. We're great friends now.'

It was such a pleasure for me, a real people person, emailing and chatting to women from all over – and everyone had a story. There was quite a big uptake from Scotland, I noticed, as word spread among its fishing communities.

I was very moved by the experiences of one lady, Helen, who lived up in Scotland but was from Yorkshire originally. She had lost her fisherman too. Their wedding in 2010 had marked a new start for the two of them, both single parents, and they were planning to go on honeymoon later in the year. But before that Graeme went back to work, away on a trawler for a trip lasting a few days. He loved the sea, his grandfather was a fisherman and he was always itching to get back out there, Helen said. But while aboard the trawler, Graeme was found dead in his bunk by his shipmates. He was diabetic, and it's thought he had some sort of attack related to that. He and Helen had been married just eight days, and Graeme was only 40 years old, a father of three. It was heartbreaking. Helen had been supported by the Fishermen's Mission in the aftermath of the tragedy, and had actually raised quite a bit of money for them already, so it felt like she really connected with what we were about.

Also from over the border was Morna, a red-headed Scot. She'd been just a little girl when her father, Donnie, went over the back of his boat. It's very easy to get lost overboard on a big boat: there are so many ropes, and you've only got to get your leg caught. It is deadly. They never found his body. Now a young woman in her twenties, she was into writing, acting, all sorts. She also had a beautiful folk voice, and turned out to be incredibly talented. Not only did she sing like an angel, she also played the harp, the flute, the piano and the fiddle, among other things. Morna had even written a play, inspired by her experience and those of the wider community, called *Lost At Sea*, and was really going places. I found her so impressive.

Hastings, just as Jackie had promised, came up with another big contingent – perhaps no wonder, given the Sussex town's long fishing history. Jackie, Didge, her daughter Toni, another Toni who we called, Toni A, Tracey, Sharyn, Mandy, Barb – the names kept coming! All in all, we had eight ladies sign up, all from families who fished on the Hastings or East Sussex coast: wives, sisters, daughters. I never quite got my head round how they all knew each other, but it seemed everyone was related in some way and it did make me smile. And I didn't want anyone to be put off just because they weren't online, so when I was doing my radio spots I would tell interested women to ring their local Fishermen's Mission outposts for details, which brought in some older ladies from places like Fleetwood, Blackpool and Scarborough.

As a result, by May 2012, just a month after making my first Facebook post about the Fishwives, the list of potential choir members numbered around 80. I felt excited, but a little nervous too. It was growing far beyond my family's story: almost without exception, everyone knew a fisherman who had been taken by the sea. I felt the burden of expectation weigh on me, as this little idea I'd had to sell a few CDs down the pub seemed to take on a life of its own. What had I unleashed?

I didn't know. But I did sense that I was on the brink of something special.

A Song of the Sea

With a last rattle of the keyboard, it was done. Sitting back from my screen, I flexed my tired fingers and gave the email I'd just written a final scan. 'Thank you so very much for your interest in joining the Fishwives Choir,' it began. 'I'm sorry this is rather a long letter but there's quite a bit to cover.' Wasn't there just! But I thought I had explained everything. I'd set out our goal – 'to record and release a single, the profits of which will go to the Fishermen's Mission' – and given all the details of how the other women could help me meet press requests for interviews, my plans for rehearsals, and how we'd best stay in contact.

It was important that I got this right: it was my very first newsletter to the Fishwives. Just keeping everyone informed of what I was planning became quite a task, I reflected. I had my list of ladies – the wives, widows, daughters, aunts, mothers and even grandmothers of fishermen, from the Scottish Highlands to the Channel Islands and everywhere in between – and they all seemed to have questions for me. I was spending days on the phone, talking through our plans, getting their details. A newsletter would save me some time, I'd decided, although I was already making mental calculations as to how many copies I'd have to print out, ready to post to those ladies who didn't have access to the internet. Indeed, on top of a full-time job and looking after small children, my life was becoming a daily round of emails, interviews and logistics. But it was no hardship: I felt full of purpose and something inside me just knew I could make it all happen. I really felt this project was blessed by God.

Still, I laugh now when I reread that first Fishwives newsletter: I sound really on top of it all. The reality was that I had no idea how to proceed with so many people, so spread out. How would the girls scattered over Cornwall get to rehearse with the ladies from Northern Ireland? I realised, too, that in my enthusiasm to include everyone, it hadn't entered my head to ask if anyone could sing or had any choir experience. In fact, I'd been telling people that being able to sing didn't matter: 'We're about the heart not the chart.' I hoped the girls could get together in smaller regional groups to practise, I explained. I planned to post the lyrics and music to people at home, or email them as music files, so they could learn their parts.

The only thing I needed was, well, the song.

At least I knew what I wanted from the start: for us not just to do a straight recording of a familiar tune, but to create our own unique song which combined music from the fields of fishing and faith.

I gravitated instantly to one of my old favourites, 'When the Boat Comes In'. A lot of people know it as the theme tune of a BBC TV series of the same name, and it has also been used in TV ads for fish products – but really it's a very old song, thought to originate from the fishing communities in the north-east, although, like many of these things, lots of people might claim it. It's all about what happens when the fishermen return, and it's a time of celebration – 'dance for your daddy' – and food (fish, of course).

I also loved the hymn 'Eternal Father' or, as it's known to many, 'For Those in Peril on the Sea', which we'd sung at my wedding and, later, at Colin's funeral. To me, that's the song of the fisherman, of every waterman. There was no question in my mind: those were our two songs.

The only thing was, 'When the Boat Comes In' and 'Eternal Father' have completely different rhythms and totally different personalities. The first is a foot-stomping folk song, the other a sombre and considered hymn. Still, I just thought that it might work. What I did was record myself singing 'Eternal Father', just using my mobile phone. Then I played that recording back to myself and tried to sing 'When the Boat Comes In' along with it, weaving in snippets, and blending my live voice with the version on my phone. I don't know what it must have looked like, me singing along to my phone. But I was thrilled: it 'fitted'!

I don't read music, however, so I had to find someone who could make this work on the page, who could translate my vision into a score. I asked Amelia's clarinet teacher if he knew anyone who could assist me in arranging a piece of music and he gave me the number of a bloke called John, a local music teacher. He agreed to help me out and did an incredible job, weaving the two separate songs together so they worked as a single piece of music. Still, I'll never forget the day when, weeks later, he came round to unveil the fruit of his efforts.

'Here you go, Jane,' he said, revealing dozens of printed pages. I looked at them and my heart sank – it was a music score, hundreds of notes winding up and down a stave. And I had no idea how to read them.

'That's brilliant, that's perfect,' I said, thinking, how the hell does this go? I didn't want to hurt his feelings by telling him that all his efforts might be in vain.

But I realised I had to come clean.

'I, er, don't really read music that well,' I admitted.

'Oh, well, you know it goes like this,' said John, and started attempting to explain what the pages and pages of score should sound like.

'Oh, okay.' I nodded along – but I didn't really understand what it all meant. Still, at least I now *had* our song, even if I hadn't a clue how to read it.

I turned to my friend Ian, another pal from the musical community. Bingo. It wasn't easy, but we came up with a plan. What Ian did was make a backing track, then I hired a professional singer to go into a studio and sing all the different parts of John's arrangement, recorded onto a CD. There were four solo parts and a role for the chorus – the bulk of the choir – so it was quite a complicated piece of music. Nobody was singing the same thing at the same time. My thinking was that this way the choir members could learn their parts by following the recording, rather than attempting to read the written music score.

But are things ever that straightforward? The problem

was that the lady was a choral singer – technically brilliant – but that gives a very specific, polished sound. We're never going to be able to achieve that! I thought. Plus, although she had performed each part separately, they were all mixed into one track. If you've got five parts sung by the same voice, it's quite hard for the untrained ear to pick out what they're supposed to be singing. I realised what this all meant when we got into rehearsal mode – after another bit of a misstep.

I'd tried to get everyone to rehearse together by video link on their computers, you see. Gathering everyone from Scotland to Cornwall in one spot to practise just wasn't realistic, so this was my solution. Maybe it wasn't ideal, but at least it meant those women who could get online could have a bash at singing together.

The reality was a bit different. That evening, as more and more fishwives-in-training started signing up to our video link, I could see it was not going to go as I had hoped. In front of me on my screen were loads of little squares showing ladies' faces, all freezing at different points, everyone experiencing slightly different time delays over the link-up, and half of them shouting, 'I can't hear!' and 'Am I plugged in, love?' One woman was even standing behind her ironing board!

I fell about laughing. But it was definitely time to move the project beyond phone calls and emails and bite the bullet – I needed to book a rehearsal.

I rang John, who'd arranged our song.

'John, I'm stuck. I don't really know what to do next. I

know we've got to rehearse, but I just wondered if you had any ideas about the best way to make it happen?'

'Oh yes,' he said, 'I play the organ in church in Shoebury and they have a lovely little hall that I'm sure they would let us use. Let me check with them and tell you what dates are available and get back to you as soon as I can.'

He was as good as his word, and so our first rehearsal was booked for half-term: 27 October 2012.

Practice Makes Perfect?

'Well done, Jane! You've a good crowd here,' said John. 'Now shall we get on with it?'

I took a deep breath. 'Ready as we'll ever be!'

Around me, the flurry of excited greetings continued. There must be a dozen of us here today, I thought; mostly local, of course, for this, the Fishwives' first rehearsal, but one lady, Barbara, had come all the way from Plymouth. Another, also called Barbara, was part of the Hastings group. Hastings Barbara would be 'Barb', we'd decided, to keep things simple.

'Ahem!' It was John, beckoning everyone to the chairs we'd set out earlier. Feeling a flutter of nerves, I joined the group as we all took a seat, carrying on our hushed introductions.

'Hello, ladies,' he began, 'it's lovely to meet you all. Now, who's alto, soprano or falsetto?'

We all looked blankly at him. I knew he was referring to the different vocal ranges, but I'd no idea what types of voices we had among us!

Then Barbara piped up: 'I usually sing soprano but if I can have the alto parts highlighted as well, please, I could try those too?'

Didge, another of the Hastings lot, leant over to me. 'Blimey,' she whispered, 'at least there's one of us here who's done this before!'

I was very impressed that Barbara knew what she was talking about.

'Yeah,' I replied quietly, 'I'm going to make sure I sit beside her next time!'

Didge laughed and John continued. 'Right, ladies, we have three hours, so let's make a start. How far have you got already learning this at home?'

I glanced around – more blank looks.

Not to be beaten, John carried on: 'Ah, not to worry, I've taught plenty of beginners. Okay, let's get into groups. Who's sung *anything* before?'

And so he sorted us into groups of beginners and the more experienced, and we all listened to the track a couple of times. He started to encourage us to sing along, giving us cues and signalling when we should join in. It began to make more sense to us all – although the actual sound we were making left something to be desired.

I listened carefully. What was going on here? Someone was supposed to be singing a line from the folk song, 'You shall have a fishy on a little dishy' – repeated – while somebody else sang a line from the hymn, 'Eternal Father, strong to save.' But because people had struggled to identify the different elements on the recording I sent out to everyone, they were muddling it all up and ending up singing something more like: 'You shall have a fishy / Eternal Father.' Something, it was clear, had been lost in translation.

But even if it wasn't totally smooth sailing, I was on a high. For me, simply being in that room was a joy: buoyed by my sessions with the singing coach, I was again finding myself able to push past my block about singing, to avoid being reduced to tears after just a few notes. This time, I think because I was in organising mode, and because this was part of a project, it just didn't act as that emotional trigger. John was there, the new girls were looking to me. I felt I was at the helm, with everyone turning to me to pull it all together. So I just got on with it.

As the first rehearsal drew to an end we all hugged, said our goodbyes and pencilled in a date the following week for the next session.

Staying behind afterwards to help tidy up, I turned to John. 'Well, how do you think it went?'

'Onwards and upwards,' he replied. 'It'll all just take a bit of practice.'

He was very diplomatic!

But back home, as I uploaded some of the photos I'd taken on my phone onto our Fishwives Facebook page, I couldn't help but smile at what I saw – all these excited faces, new and old. And I was very touched by those ladies who had travelled so far to be part of the first session.

The next day, while I was at work, I had a call from a regional TV show. They were keen to do a story on us. Impulsively, I invited the news team to our next rehearsal. But as I hung up, I had a moment of clarity. What the hell had I done? There was no way we'd be ready to sing on television in six days – was there?

I rang John again.

'Er, John...' I began. I wasn't sure how he'd take the news! But he had a plan.

'We'll concentrate on getting one section as good as possible,' he said.

I emailed all the girls to let them know that a TV crew would be filming us at the next rehearsal. Three of the Leigh ladies replied saying they were ever so sorry but, having given the project more thought, they couldn't commit to weekly rehearsals – but wished us lots of luck. I understood completely, but I was a bit worried about our forthcoming rehearsal being a bit sparsely populated by Essex girls. So, I made a call and persuaded 'Auntie' Sandra to come. She was related – albeit distantly – to the Dolby fishing family, but long before we discovered there was a family connection, Sandra and I were already friends.

Colin had known her husband Gareth, a keen sailor, for years and Sandra and her sister Anne had shown me and the children incredible kindness in the weeks after Colin was missing, lavishing us with care, good food and support. Their whole family had made sure they were there on Henry's, Amelia's and Liam's birthdays, which all took place within a month or so of losing Colin. I was so glad to have them in our lives. Since discovering our family connection, Sandra had started calling me 'Auntie Jane' for a joke. In return I called her 'Auntie Sandra' – and somehow it stuck.

Soon we were back in the little church hall ready for our second rehearsal.

'All set?' I greeted everyone as they filed through the doors. 'Now the cameras are arriving in two hours. So, John, you've got a little while to try to get us into shape!'

'I like a challenge,' he said with a smile, walking over to the piano.

There was a wail. 'Oh for God's sake, Auntie Jane, you *know* I can't sing.'

It was Sandra, arriving with an enormous bag on her shoulder and a bobble hat pulled down over her short plum-coloured hair.

'What on earth have you got in there?' asked Laura, one of our other Leigh girls, wide-eyed.

Sitting down, Sandra placed her bag on a neighbouring chair and started pulling out a flask of tea, a lunchbox of snacks and balls of wool. It was like when Mary Poppins pulls pot plants and lampshades out of her magical handbag – it just kept coming!

'Auntie Sandra, you're supposed to be singing, not knitting,' I reminded her.

'Look, dear' – waving my concerns away with a flick of her hand – 'I said I'd come to help you make the numbers up. I may not be able to sing but I can mime brilliantly.'

And she began clicking her needles ten to the dozen and mouthing in an exaggerated fashion, 'Eternal father, strong to save.'

'See,' she said, 'I really don't know what you're worried about!'

I had to laugh. Sandra was a real eccentric and I loved her for it.

We worked hard as John put us through our paces, then stopped for a tea break.

'Well, I'm really enjoying myself,' said Lee, munching one of the cakes the Hastings girls had brought. 'But I don't know how choir-like we sound. We'll get prosecuted under trade descriptions!'

'Don't know how choir-like we sound *yet*,' corrected John, ever the optimist. 'You'll get there.'

'Well, I think we sound bleedin' pucker already,' said Lara, our lady from Leigh's cockle sheds. Lara was a real character – a fascinating mixture of salt of the earth and spiritual seeker. Once, I interrupted a conversation she was having with our producer Phil.

'What are you two yakking about?'

'Oh, you know,' she said casually in her broad Estuary twang, 'quantum physics and house music.' That summed her up perfectly.

The BBC crew arrived during our tea break and off we went. We did as we were instructed – 'Can you sing that part again?' – and the presenter interviewed me in a side room. I told my story, explaining the purpose of the choir, and then returned to the rest of the throng to join them in a final chorus. We weren't pitch-perfect as the cameras rolled, but the idea was more about explaining what we were hoping to do than showing off a finished performance.

After the TV crew left, I headed into the hall's kitchen to make more tea. I could hear some of the Hastings girls' conversations.

'We definitely sounded better that time,' said one.

'I'm still very confused.'

'You're always confused!'

The session was over all too soon. We pencilled in another rehearsal date, wished each other all the best, and promised faithfully to practise like mad at home.

I knew, though, that our lack of experience was an issue. In a choir, even if people do know their part, if you've got someone who's not used to singing, as soon as you put them next to somebody singing a different part they will start following that one: they can't hold their own tune. It's just something that comes with practice.

The line-up was changing, too. People had other commitments, realised the work that would be required; perhaps it wasn't for some. And more and more women were still writing to me, wanting to be part of it. The upshot was that there was almost a complete refreshment of that line-up during the course of our rehearsals. I think just Lee, Laura and her friend Holly, who was also married to a fisherman, and I were the constants.

Still, we persevered, continuing with rehearsals over the following months – and if we weren't making much progress, we were getting to know each other, and having a ball.

Move Over, Bob Geldof!

Much as I was enjoying myself, I could see that if the rehearsals weren't running smoothly, actually recording this thing was going to be difficult. The latest idea I'd cooked up was to get a backing track recorded, post this on CD to the various women, and get a recording studio in every area to donate their free time. The ladies in their separate local groups would then be recorded, I'd have to get the tracks emailed to me, and find a producer to mix it all together. If worst came to worst, I'd have to do it myself, I thought. It still didn't cross my mind that anybody might have to travel anywhere!

But if I sound gung-ho, I was wise enough to get some advice on my plan. That's when I approached Phil Da Costa, a songwriter and producer who had mixed the Military Wives album *In My Dreams*, which had gone to number one in the charts. I knew him already, because he'd written a couple of tracks for a young artist I'd been helping with her PR, and I'd met him a few times at gigs. He was one of the first people I'd emailed after we lost Colin, saying: 'I'm going to be out of action for a little while, my husband's just died.'

Of course, he rang – 'I'm so sorry, Jane, what can I

do?' – and we'd stayed in touch. So, when I had the idea for the Fishwives, I emailed him about the project and told him that I was going out of my comfort zone. 'Could you give me any hints about how to record the choir?'

After a couple of days, he replied: 'I'll produce it for you.' Hurrah! Another day passed and he was in touch again: 'Even better news – Jon Cohen has agreed to come and help as well.'

Shit! I thought. Jon was the Brit Award-winning producer behind the Military Wives and he was going to give up his time to come to Hastings to record this and I'm making it all up as I go along? I felt more than a little panicked, but I knew how great it would be for the project.

Still, what I wouldn't fully appreciate until later was the scale of the blessing Phil and Jon represented. My original idea to get people in local groups to record a track, then to have all the various versions mixed together by a producer, wasn't a bad one – but it was not practical. As I was soon to learn, good choir-singing requires everyone to finish their words at exactly the same time, to hold their notes together and to take breaths in unison. Without all this, songs sound messy and untidy. And it's something that can really only be achieved when you've everyone together in the same room, singing together, and listening together.

With Phil and Jon on board, everything started to crystallise. Phil said, 'These are the dates we can do' – the last week in April – and I thought, right, there's no way my original plan of recording everyone locally is going to happen. With less than two months to go, there's no chance I am going to be able to organise separate studios all round the country. I'm just going to find a studio, book it, tell everybody what we're doing, and those that can come, can come; those that can't, can't. Happily nearly half the ladies on my list could make it: there'd be more than three dozen fishwives in that recording studio, I calculated.

Then we had another stroke of luck. Years ago, I'd met a vocal coach called Tommy through my music work, and I'd stayed in contact, letting her know what I was up to. 'I've set up this choir,' I told her, 'and a lot of us don't have very much singing experience. Do you know of any online vocal tuition that you could recommend for us to do in our own time?'

Now, Tommy and her friend Sarah both sang professionally and ran a company, Globe Jam, that offers singing workshops in offices and other institutions – community singing experts, you could call them.

'I tell you what, I'll talk to Sarah and see if we can make you a tutorial,' she said – and they did: they made three videos for us, which we could all watch on YouTube.

'Hello, Fishwives!' they began, standing by a piano. That first one was about posture and breathing. 'You need your feet about shoulder-width apart ... Moving up to your knees, you don't want them completely locked, you want a slight bend in them.' Then it was centring the pelvis, relaxing the shoulders, keeping the head steady. And that was before we even got to the singing! They were so thorough, it was brilliantly helpful.

After that, from time to time Tommy would message me,

checking in about how we were getting on; and when I had the dates for our recording fixed, she casually mentioned, 'Well, if you need any help, Sarah and I could come along.' Did I ever? I jumped at the chance.

Nonetheless, preparing to go into the studio felt a bit like when you begin to decorate a room. You start off thinking, I'm just taking that wallpaper off, and then you think, oh, I didn't realise that great big crack was there. The more work you do, the more you realise there is to do! In the same way, I'd thought: I'll hire a recording studio. I found one in Hastings, where a lot of the fishwives-to-be were based, and that was that – or so I reckoned.

I had no idea until I got the ball rolling what I had to get to grips with. This was a very different business from running off those copies of my songs on CD all those years ago. I didn't know about barcodes, publishing rights, setting things up legally. To produce a single, it's not just a question of creating the CD – you have to register with various industry bodies; if the song is going to be commercially available there's a licence fee you have to pay; there's some sort of coding that is automatically picked up during airplay and registered for the charts; all sorts. I didn't even know you had to do it, let alone *how* to do it, until I started looking online. So I just did what I'd done before when I'd been presented with a challenge: cracked on with my research, then got down to it. I even sorted out contracts for the Fishwives to sign – I found them online and tweaked them to suit. We'd all agreed that the single was for charity, but I thought I'd better get that on the

Jane Dolby

record, somehow. It was crossing the 't's and dotting the 'i's, to make sure that everything was covered.

But it all cost money. I didn't know how I was going to pay for the studio, or the CD duplication, or the artwork, or anything. I didn't even know how I was going to get all the girls there. Of those women who could make the dates set for our recording, some couldn't afford the transport to get down there; and I certainly couldn't pay for them. To make the Fishwives happen, I'd already cut down my hours at work to the bare minimum I needed to cover my rent and my bills. Yet I couldn't have done anything else, I reasoned. If I hadn't squeezed my hours, I wouldn't have seen the kids at all. I couldn't give up the choir; I couldn't give up my job; and I certainly couldn't spend less time with the kids. It was a compromise I had to make and the thing that had to go was a little extra time at work and, as a result, any spare cash.

My solution? To turn into Bob Geldof. I phoned round the hotels in the Hastings area and one of them, a little B&B, gave us a really good deal. It had a little bar, too, I saw, where we could hang out together after rehearsals and recording and get to know each other, which I felt would be really important in terms of how we performed together. (And I sorted out childcare for myself: one of the lovely ladies from school, whose son Liam was friendly with, would look after him while I was away; while my old friend Angee would look after Amelia.) I started crowd-funding, too – setting up a page online to raise money from friends, family and, I hoped, other well-wishers. 'In

215

April, we will meet for the first time to record our single,' the website read. 'Ladies related to fishermen, including mums, sisters, aunts, cousins, daughters and even grans, are travelling to East Sussex from all over the UK for rehearsals and recording. Many of these ladies have lost men to the sea.' I made sure it got mentions when we gave interviews and people really responded – even complete strangers were helping us out.

In the end, we raised just over £2,000 that way to cover our costs. The Hastings girls, with typical enthusiasm, raised another couple of thousand, organising raffles and staging a Rod Stewart tribute night, and people donated their services for free. To the penny, we just had enough money to do it all: the recording, paying for flights for the girls from Scotland, everyone's petrol, the B&B. And I did the promotion so we didn't have to get a PR company. All in all, the whole thing cost about half the price it should have done. And I liked doing it, keeping everything going, organising and encouraging. Never mind going on stage, perhaps this was what I've always gravitated towards, I thought, even back in my days putting on carnivals as a child and bossing the other kids around!

If the logistics of getting dozens of women into a recording studio were on track, I was less sure about what would happen once we were in there. I'd planned for us to have five days in Hastings, three rehearsing, then two in the studio. But I didn't know how the ladies would be able to hold harmonies, I didn't know how much time we'd have trying to hold intricate melodies. While some women were quite experienced singers who could sight-read a music score, it was more often the case that they hadn't sung since their school days.

Then, with just a week to go, before we got to Hastings, Phil Da Costa asked me, 'Who's MD-ing it?' – who was looking after the musical direction?

'What do you mean?' I said.

'Well, when you get there, who's going to run the rehearsals?'

It was at that point it dawned on me. Those who'd made it to our local rehearsals were having a real struggle learning this song over the past few months, and still hadn't got it right. We'd get to Hastings, we would have even more women – and just 48 hours to get it down pat.

Oh God, I thought, we've all been learning it for months and the rest will only have two days! I was filled with total panic. I've got Phil and Jon who've worked with the Military Wives, all these ladies coming. How is it going to happen?

That's when I turned to my eldest son Josh to help, even though he'd never done anything like that before. Always musical, he'd gone on to study composition at university and spent his working life now composing scores or DJ-ing in Berlin where he lived. Conducting a choir full of women wasn't something he'd tackled before.

'Please will you help us?' I asked him.

'Well all right, I suppose it won't be too different from conducting an orchestra,' he said.

Yeah, I thought – an orchestra that has never read music

or played an instrument before! 'Mm, yes, yes, it will be,' I said, 'it'll be fine, you'll love it!'

But at least that was sorted: he would look after the music in that respect.

Was it luck, how everything was finally falling into place – or something else? I didn't stop and think about it, not then, at least. You see, I'd spent the last few years helping young artists release singles and putting on events, helping musicians. And so, as more people made contact, my vision of the project was just growing incrementally, a little every day. There wasn't a spare moment to sit back and reflect on what was happening.

Ready or not, we Fishwives were on our way.

A Turning Point

As the last piano chords died away, the low buzz of excited chatter started up again. Our first day rehearsing as the Fishwives was proving to be an absolute blast. You might expect it to have been a sombre occasion, we being a group of women brought together by shared danger and loss. Not a bit of it. I'd driven down to Hastings in a car with a couple of the other Essex girls – Lee and Lara – and from the moment the engine had started it was as if we'd all known each other for ever. Our spirits had risen even higher as we met up in a beautiful building, a former church-turned-arts venue, sorted by Jackie from Hastings. We'd walked into a flurry of excited greetings as three dozen women gathered around the grand piano and started putting faces to the names many of them had only seen over email for the last few months. 'Hello, how are you?' 'How was your journey?' 'I recognise *you*!'

The thing was, when I'd been getting everybody involved, we'd shared our stories, our experiences: over the phone, over email, over Facebook. I'd told them about Colin, sent the local press coverage from when his boat went missing – 'This is my story, this is what I'm doing it for,' 'I'm so sorry, I knew someone too, I lost my brother' – and so we'd had those conversations before we'd even met. By the time we did get to see each other in person, we just wanted to have fun, enjoy the moment and talk about the future – especially that first day. I was just revelling in meeting these people I'd been communicating with long-distance for the past few months. Already there were people I batted texts and emails around with; whom I'd clicked with even online.

We had such a great range of women in that room, I thought, as I scanned the smiling faces. The youngest was my cousin's daughter Sarah, by now in her early twenties. While she'd become a doctor, working up in Edinburgh, she was also a music teacher and a talented musician – a grade-eight pianist – with a beautiful voice. Her connection was through me, of course; she was related to Colin by marriage. The oldest was a lovely lady from Northern Ireland in her seventies; her sons, husband and grandfather were all, or had been, in the fishing industry. Immediately, I could see friendships being forged. I smiled to myself. The Celts, in particular, were already getting on like a house on fire. We had a couple of Welsh girls, a couple of Cornish girls and a few from Devon and Ireland, and they were all sitting together, as if they naturally gravitated towards each other. The Essex and Hastings girls also seemed to be bonding. It was marvellous to see.

There was more excitement that day, as a crew from *The One Show*, the BBC magazine programme, was coming to film us. The plan suggested by the producers was that Carrie Grant would offer us vocal coaching, and I'd nearly bitten their hand off. She was the vocal coach who'd worked on programmes like *Fame Academy*, and was unbelievably good at what she did, I knew. From the moment that she and the crew walked through the door, Carrie instantly recognisable with that fabulous red hair, she set us all at ease: so friendly and warm. I was already feeling fairly confident, too. I knew there was a lot of work ahead in getting the songs to recording standard, but we'd have Tommy and Sarah, our vocal coaches, down later in the week, and all these other great people around to support us. Alison, the lady who looked after fundraising at the Fishermen's Mission, even came down and made a little speech to thank everybody. People do all sorts for the Mission – fun runs, marathons, throw themselves out of aeroplanes – but they hadn't done this before.

Still, if, technically, we were getting there as Carrie started putting us through our paces – hitting our notes, trotting through our harmonies with precision – I had to admit there was still something, well, lacking. But what? Here was I, a normal housewife, miles from home with more than three dozen other women who were just as – if not more – out of their depth.

'Ladies, ladies' – a voice rose over the buzz, Carrie again. But now she wasn't talking about breathing or harmonies or rhythm, or anything to do with the technical side of it at all.

'My favourite lines that you've sung so far are: "Oh hear us when we cry to Thee / For those in peril on the sea," ' she told us. 'You've all got stories and a history to tell – you are so connected to this song, in a way that people who don't have that history aren't.'

Now she really had our attention. 'When you sing that line,' she said, 'that's got to mean something to you – it's got to cost you.'

And that was the moment. That was when it finally hit us: the reality of what that song meant to us. What had the sea cost us? We all knew; we couldn't have been more painfully aware of it. It was what we had to live with every day as the wives, sisters and mothers of fishermen: the threat of the sea's power, the dangers it presented, the losses it could wreak. We couldn't escape it – that was why we were all there.

Once more, the piano started up again with the familiar tune; once more, we readied for the first deep intake of breath, poised to fill our lungs to sustain the sound we were reaching for. But this time, something shifted. As we started to sing that song again, everything had changed. As our voices swelled together, goose bumps prickled up my arms. Every woman present had simply started singing it very differently – me included. We were all there for the same cause, and for the first time we really connected to that.

Finally, in that room with the other women, the reality of what we'd done hit me, what we were going to achieve, what those words meant for me – singing a song that combined a prayer for those in peril on the sea with a message to the little laddie waiting for his daddy to come home. I had a little laddie, and his daddy was never going to come home. I was overcome by a feeling of utter release;

of opening the floodgates. Carrie's words had unlocked something within me, within us all, and it was wonderful. As the last notes died away, I burst into tears. I looked around; my feelings were reflected on every face I saw – my tears shared by every woman in the room.

'Yeah,' said Carrie. 'Now you're singing.'

That was a turning point – for the choir, and for me. Through it all, I'd never felt that Colin was 'looking out for me', anything like that – but that day I did feel something: I truly felt that this project was bigger than all of us.

Later, I texted Carrie: 'I feel better than I've felt for ages, I feel liberated.' For what I didn't know then was that that day really would have lasting effects. Those lessons with my singing teacher had helped, yes. I could get the words out again. But what that day – singing with all the Fishwives – did was place my love of music well and truly back at the heart of my life, as a source of huge joy and release for me. Today I am completely freed from any emotional block on my voice – I sing along in the car, in the shower, with the radio. Try and stop me! What a gift it was for me to be able to sing again. There really is a healing power to music that nourishes my soul.

High Tide in Hastings

'Wait, wait, hold on, don't start without me!'

Down the stony beach, wearing the highest shoes you have ever seen, tottered Lisa. My favourite glamazon was all made up in six-inch heels and a beautiful turquoise top.

'Help!' she cried. 'I've got problems with my shoes, I keep sinking!'

Only Lisa would think of wearing shoes fit for a night-club on a pebble beach, but she wasn't one to admit defeat. Finally reaching us, she took a spot among the Fishwives, and beamed.

'Right, ladies, are we all ready for our close-up?'

Our week in Hastings was continuing to be a whirlwind. Today, a reporter and photographer from a national news-paper had come down to see what was going on and take some pictures of us on the town's beach. I'd managed to get all the girls ready in place, and everyone had dutifully worn a blue top so we looked like a proper group.

'Oh, buggeration,' I said to Laura under my breath, as we grouped in rows, 'I didn't think to tell anyone to wear a particular shade.'

'No, it's perfect,' said Laura. 'All those different shades of blue – it's just like the sea!'

I gazed again at the women around us. She was right: together we looked just right. A real team.

Really, I think I was on a high all that week, surrounded by my friends old and new.

I was so proud of my son Josh, taking charge of the musical direction; he was patient with everybody and really encouraging. The ladies all said he was like their security blanket, that they didn't think they could have done it without him. And I had another familiar face in John, who'd arranged our song, and was to play the piano as we rehearsed, which was lovely.

Later we were joined by Tommy and Sarah, our long-distance vocal coaches. Everyone said that they felt like they knew them already when they met, because they'd been watching them for ages via the YouTube videos they'd made for us. But working with the pair of them in person just couldn't be replicated. They'd be listening to our harmonies, checking that people were singing in their correct range, making sure everyone was singing with the proper open mouth; getting the technique right. If someone was going off-track one of them would go and stand next to her, singing her part nice and loud, so that she could follow her lead. And so, as the hours ticked by, we started really making strides.

I loved getting into the studio at the end of the week: I've always felt completely comfortable in the studio, gathering round our shared mics, putting on our headphones.

It's so different to being on stage – you can make mistakes, say, 'Can I do that again?' And I felt still more reassured singing with the other Fishwives. When you're young and in a band, reaching for the stars, if you make a mistake tempers can flare: 'What the hell have you done that for, you messed it up!' But we weren't like that; it was, 'Oh don't worry about it, who cares?' There were no egos at stake. Everybody was in it together, for something bigger than themselves.

I learnt too, seeing Phil and Jon in action, that being a producer is not just about having good ears. It's about being massively skilled in dealing with people. So much of singing or playing music is about what's in your mind – if you think you can do it, you can. But if you hit a bum note or keep forgetting your part, it really doesn't take much before you say to yourself: I can't do this. And then the doubts set in. You start telling yourself, I'm wasting everybody's time, we're on a tight schedule here – and as soon as you're in that negative mental cycle, you can't perform properly.

Fortunately for us all, they had spectacular skills in making us think we could do it. If somebody says, 'I can't hit that note,' and somebody replies, 'Yes, you can' – that's actually no help at all. But if somebody responds, 'Why don't you try sliding into that; those two notes before that one, that's the one that you want to hit again' – gives you specific instructions – you can really perform.

In that way, they knew how to get the best out of us. If someone made a mistake, it would be: 'Don't worry about it, we'll go back to it,' or 'Terrific, let's do it again, I want to get a few recordings of this' – and actually it hadn't been terrific at all, but they'd not let you know.

They were a great double act, too – funny, terrific at keeping the mood light. At one point Jon put all the deeper-voiced ladies together, to add the bass notes on the recording: me, Lara, Joy from Devon, Esther, and Keri and Rachel from Wales. 'We're the Daves!' we'd joke, because we had lower-pitched voices. 'Cue the Daves!' Just silliness, but oh, it made us laugh. Phil, in particular, I got to know: gentle, funny, he could also be candid when it's called for. There are not many relationships where someone can tell you, 'This isn't right, Jane, you're not singing your best, your diction's not on,' and you can trust the motivation. All the Fishwives benefited from his instruction and he was really good fun too, all the girls loved him.

The music side was just the half of it, though. We had so much media interest that week: TV stations, local press, national newspapers, yet more radio people. The itinerary was to the minute: we've a rehearsal, then a break, that will give just enough time for so-and-so to do an interview while the rest of us are photographed on the beach, then it's back into rehearsal. There really was not a spare second, from eight o'clock in the morning to nine o'clock at night, it was filled with interviews, rehearsals, then recording sessions. At one point Phil – always the steady head – reminded me: 'I know you've organised all this press coverage, but you must remember we've got to be in that studio!' Because it was easy for us to get caught up in the excitement of publicity, and I did feel like a headmistress sometimes – 'You've got two minutes and you've got to be back in' – bossing everybody around!

It helped, I think, that I kept feeling like I was doing one of my publicity projects for a singer or a band – and forgetting that it was mine. That was probably quite handy in keeping me calm. For there was so much going on. I'd had a call from Simon Hanning, who'd recently made the video for a cover version of the Hollies hit 'He Ain't Heavy, He's My Brother', released as a tribute to the Hillsborough tragedy. Again, I knew him through my music connections. 'I'll come and make your music video, no charge, I'll just donate my time,' he said. 'But,' he added, 'I can only come on that last day' – the Friday, which was when loads of TV cameras were coming to film us in the studio. It was absolutely mad. One TV crew turned up and I didn't even know they were coming. At one point, I remember saying to Lisa over a cup of tea: 'This has been the most incredible adventure, but I'm so knackered that in a way I'll be glad to get my life back to normal when we get home – won't you lot?'

'Well, I quite like this life.' She laughed. 'I think being a rock star would suit me!'

That wasn't all. Just before we went to Hastings, I'd had a phone call from a lady I didn't know, who said her name was Minghua. 'We're very interested in the fishing community,' she said, 'we'll come to Hastings and be part of it – we'll do an interview.' In the rush of getting every-thing ready, I hadn't quite grasped where she was from, but we already had a lot of press coming down. The more the merrier was my attitude by now.

'Okay,' I said, 'here's our itinerary.' I didn't expect these two ladies to show up and stay! It turned out that Minghua and her colleague Esther were academics from the Greenwich Maritime Institute in London, doing highbrow research into women in coastal communities and the sociology of it all. It was a serious piece of work being carried out across Europe – and here are we, I thought, just singing and having a few drinks in the evenings!

'We just need half an hour with each person,' they said to me.

Oh dear, I thought, every minute is accounted for.

'Look,' I said, 'we won't have time for that, really. Why don't you just join the choir? Sing on the single, be part of it, and write about it from that perspective.' So, as it turned out, Minghua had to go back to London, but Esther could stay for the week – and did.

We all loved her. This tall Colombian woman – British-Colombian by this point, as she'd been living in the UK a while – was very attractive and dignified, and so clever; she had about four degrees, it seemed to me. She was so up for it, but at the same time it was so outside her comfort zone and you could tell that, at first, she was doing it as an act of research. She's since explained to me in a bit more detail why she got involved. The project she was working on was trying to enhance women's contribution to the fisheries sector, not just as fishwives – wives and mothers of fishermen – but in terms of the wider 'cultural heritage'.

She'd been working in Japan and Africa, all over the world, and said that development in coastal areas, she'd noticed, tended to come from women. So it's women driving these communities forward, keeping them going, I thought.

Her taking part had even been given the status of 'participatory observation', apparently. But it became more than research, I could tell. It was wonderful to see her inhibitions crumble and her joining in wholeheartedly with the rest of us, laughing and joking, especially with the Irish contingent. They just clicked.

'It's so funny, Esther,' I said to her, 'you came along to document it and ended up being part of it.'

'It wasn't an academic exercise,' she later told me. 'It came so much from your hearts that I couldn't be just an academic. There was so much truth, there was so much connection among that group of women.'

That was lovely to hear – that was just what the choir was all about.

So, there was a lot going on. But despite the whirl of it all, I didn't get tired – at least, not until I got home. In fact, I partied like anything. I think I got about two hours' sleep a night. Yes, I was working really hard, keeping everything running on schedule, but it still felt like a holiday. Since Colin had died, I'd had those five days away to do my driving course and test, and that was really it. What's more, knowing my kids were being well looked after back in Leigh, I didn't have to clock-watch. So I was like a teenager, wanting to stay up all night! I hadn't been out for ages – years; loads of my friends were there, I'd made loads more new friends, and I was full of adrenalin. People would say, 'Oh, I'm going to go to bed now,' and I would think, there's no way I'm going to bed now. And then I'd stay up until four in the morning in the B&B bar with the hardcore partyers: Lee, Lara, Sarah, Lisa, Phil, Josh and the Hastings girls. Funnily enough, it was mostly the older ones, all the younger girls turning in early. I was on such a high the whole time. I was just so happy to be there.

One evening in particular was very special. The Hastings ladies invited us all to a sea shanty night, a regular event in their town.

'I've never been to a shanty night,' I said to Lara, as a few of us Essex lot walked to the pub where it was taking place, the Stag. 'I wonder what it's like.'

'Don't ask me.' She laughed. 'I've only ever been to bleedin' raves!'

'It'll probably be a bit "I'll have a pint of beer with my finger in my ear," ' said Wendy. 'You know, folky.'

'I expect it will be really nice, though,' I said. Privately, I wasn't sure it would be quite up my street.

Inside the packed pub, the Hastings lot were already settled in for the night and beckoned us over. After a flurry of hellos and bar orders, we were chatting away when –

'Come all ye young fellows that follow the sea . . .' a strong male baritone rang out.

'To me, way hey, blow the man down!' dozens of voices roared back.

I jumped in my seat. Suddenly the whole place was alive with song.

231

'Now please pay attention and listen to me / Give me some time to blow the man down.'

What was this? Looking around the pub, I could see everyone – from the professionals who'd been downing Chardonnay to the weathered fishermen nursing their pints – was singing along. There was no stage, just a guy with an accordion accompanying the singing, and yet the whole pub was filled with music. I so wanted to be part of it too.

'Everyone knows the words except us,' I said, leaning over to Lisa.

'Oh, that doesn't matter,' she half-shouted, trying to make herself heard over the rowdy vocals. 'It's not going to stop me!'

Sure enough, all we Essex girls started 'la-la-ing' along.

Every so often there'd be a pause, then somebody new would start with the opening words to a song, and everyone would join in. They were songs with unfamiliar lyrics and stranger names – 'John Kanaka', 'Windy Old Weather' – that the seamen used to sing on the boats and round the harbours. Yet everyone seemed to know them.

Then, in the lull as one song ended, I heard a lone female voice rise out of the silence.

'Our ship went a-sailing out over the bar . . .'

And everyone joined in for the response, 'Away, for Rio!'

I skimmed the faces in the pub, trying to find the singer. To my astonishment, I saw it was none other than Joy. One of the quieter Fishwives, she was training to be a doctor and her partner was a harbour master in Clovelly in Devon.

'She's pointed her bow to the bright southern star,' Joy's rich voice rang out.

'And we're bound for the Rio Grande!' replied the crowd.

Leading this pub full of strangers in song, Joy was so confident, singing with such ease. Clearly, she'd done this before, as well.

'She's brilliant,' I said to Toni, Didge's daughter. 'This whole *idea* is absolutely brilliant!'

'Isn't it? They sing here every Thursday night.'

'Is it always this busy?'

'Yeah, it's always packed.'

That made me pause. 'We've got such a strong heritage of folk music back home in Leigh – but I'm pretty sure there are no shanty events.'

I leant over to Lee and Lara. 'Why don't we do this at home? We've a fishing history, too.'

Sitting back in my chair, I started la-la-ing along with the best of them. But my mind was whirring. I was fascinated by the idea that you could just rock up and start singing and it would be a community event – nothing to do with talent shows, or the record industry, or anything commercial at all. I didn't know it then, but that night would change the direction of my life.

Of course, over the week there were times when we did talk about our losses, and I was struck by how much gallows humour and fighting spirit there was among these women. That sounds a bit clichéd, but it's the truth. These were women who just got on with things, tried to turn their situation into something positive. And that was our common ground. It meant that there was a depth underlying everything, an emotional intimacy based on our shared experiences, even if we didn't have the long history of friendship that usually lies behind that sort of understanding. It was an intense feeling. As Morna said, 'It was like we'd all known each other for years.' I felt especially connected to those women who had experienced a similar loss to me – lost their men. Morna, who had lost her father, Helen and Sue, who had lost their husbands. That was bittersweet.

Recently, I asked a couple of the other Fishwives how they remembered it. 'It was sad, at times,' said Sue. 'But it's just so nice to speak to other people who've been in your situation – because you don't often meet people in your circumstances. The rest of the time we had a great laugh and made lots of new friends.'

And I think that really summed up the week for me – and, I hope, everyone else.

As Laura said, 'Something just clicked. We all got on really well. No one scene sticks in my mind, nothing happened, there wasn't an "event". It's just that feeling – that warm, fuzzy feeling. It was a really good connection that we all had and that will stick with me more than anything else.'

There were moments, in fact, when I was feeling so euphoric about everything – it was so incredible to be there singing our hearts out, to relax with a glass of wine afterwards, to feel connected to all these ladies – that a terrible guilt would roll over me. It's cost Colin his life for me to be this happy, I'd think, none of this would be happening if he were here. That was quite confusing for me at times, that something I so loved had come out of something so terrible. I'd have to really give myself a talking-to.

But he'd want me to be happy, I'd say to myself, he'd want me to be doing this, he'd want me to set a good example to the kids about doing the best with the hand you were dealt. He wouldn't want me to be falling apart every single day; he'd be pleased that I was doing the right thing in paying back my debts to the people who had helped me when I was at my lowest. Colin knew, too, that I lived for a project, and this was my biggest project yet. And he would have just loved it, I knew – bringing the children to see me sing. He would have been in his element.

He was always so supportive of everything I did, bless him, but he would have really liked this.

Lights, Camera, Action

'So,' asked my colleague Tom. 'How was it then? Did you have a great time?'

Lee, who was also in the choir, was his mum, so he'd heard loads about it from the two of us in the run-up.

'Oh my God, I had the most incredible time!' I said, dropping my coat on my office chair. 'But it was full-on, really non-stop. I feel absolutely shattered. I can't remember ever being so tired! But how about you? How are things?'

Then my mobile rang. It was another journalist.

Placing my hand over the receiver, I said to Tom: 'Look, I'm sorry, I've just got dash out and take this,' and I ran out to the car park to do another interview.

My boss at Southend YMCA had shown me incredible generosity; she'd placed such trust in me to deliver my work around the demands of the Fishwives. But I didn't want to push it. So, that night, I rang Lee to share my latest plan.

'I'm going to lose my job if I spend so much time doing these interviews!' I told her. 'The journalists usually want to cover the same ground. So, I'm going to write it all down, put it online, and then if a journalist asks for an interview I can point them to it – and if they need to know anything else they can ring me after six o'clock.'

'It's a really good idea,' agreed Lee. 'You can't risk your job. We're not famous yet!'

And so, over the next couple of days, I did as I'd planned. I called the blog post 'I choose happiness'. As a result, the media calls got much more manageable and I threw myself back into work and family.

But if, on the surface, real life had taken over, the Fish-wives were always at the back of my mind. I still didn't know what the finished single would sound like. When you record a song, you don't hear the final version when you're in the studio. In fact, you don't hear it back for weeks. So now Phil had to take all the different variations of our song, which we'd sung over and over, and work out which sounded best, not to mention blending in the string parts. It was a huge amount of work for him to mix that single. But at least that was not something that I had to worry about. It was back to reality for me – but not for long.

Before the single's planned release date, 28 August – Colin's birthday – Phil gave me a call.

'Just wanted to let you know that the single mix is coming on really well and will be ready for an August release, as planned,' he said. 'We need all the help we can get to publicise the song.'

It was true. We didn't have a record deal, any financial backing, management or a big marketing company behind us.

'Phil, I think our only hope of getting some publicity is to contact the journalists and regional media presenters who've been unbelievably supportive of our story so far.

Maybe, if there's enough regional interest, our single might get on the radar of the national media.'

It was back to the flurry of calls and emails, working hard to create a buzz around us.

A few weeks later, I got another call. Would we like to appear on *BBC Breakfast*?

'Of course,' I said calmly, 'we'd love to.' And as I hung up, I gave a quiet scream! This was too good an opportunity to pass up, performing on national TV just days before our single officially launched. But it did mean that, at very short notice, I had to get everybody to Manchester for filming at the BBC complex in nearby Salford. I rang all the girls to let them know.

'What?'

'Oh my GOD!'

'Count me in!'

Everyone was hugely excited. Still, there were a good few who couldn't come due to childcare or work commitments, Josh among them, and Hannah, one of our soloists.

I called Phil again. 'So, we have to reduce the song down to two and a half minutes to fit the BBC timings, and be in Manchester the day before. Would you be able to do a remix?'

'Well I can, of course – but have you thought about how you might rehearse it?'

'I've got no idea at all yet! I'm afraid the only opportunity we'll have for a rehearsal is the night before the performance. It's not ideal but it's all we've got.'

I took a deep breath. 'There's another potential problem too . . .'

'Go ahead – I'm bracing myself!'

'Okay, don't panic, but we have to cover fares and petrol for the girls who want to come, we need to pay for accommodation and because there are so many of us the BBC has to hire some equipment – and we have to cover the cost of that, too.'

It could add up to thousands of pounds, I knew.

'Blimey,' said Phil, 'well, I'll crack on with organising the music and if anyone can make the rest of the stuff happen, you can.'

'I don't know where to start really,' I admitted. 'I can't expect the girls to pay their own fares and accommodation and most of them don't have any spare money. But I'll do my best.'

After I hung up, I said a prayer: 'Lord, I don't know what your plans are for the Fishwives but I believe you've brought us this far. If you want me to give it up I will – but if you have a purpose for us please help me to get everybody to Manchester and make this happen. We are all in your hands, Lord – and I give it all over to you.'

I asked Lisa and Tim to pray, too. In the meantime – in the absence of any lightning bolts from above telling me to knock it all on the head – I planned to spend the next few days with a phone permanently attached to my ear. If it was a bit stressful, I didn't feel out of my depth in terms of making it all happen. I wasn't phased by the responsibility: I'm quite happy at the centre of an organisational whirl.

First, I googled 'hotel chains in Manchester' and started to contact them all.

'Hello,' I'd start, before launching into my spiel. 'Can you help? Yes, there are about thirty of us coming... Okay, no it's all right, don't apologise, I understand, it's a big ask. Don't worry.'

I trusted God and that if He wanted us there, we'd get there. I kept dialling. And finally I got two calls back: one from the Portland Hotel, offering all of us bed, breakfast and an evening meal, and another from a hotel called Pinewood, volunteering a spread the day after. I felt buoyed up, and kept going – we could do this!

They say good luck comes in threes – and the third lucky call was from a kindly man called Michael, from the corporate social responsibility department at Tesco.

'We'll help with the costs of equipment hire,' he said. 'Because you are not the charity, we will give it to the Fishermen's Mission and then they can donate it to you.'

Then National Express, the coach company, offered us transport to Manchester from wherever we were in the UK, even extending their offer to the Northern Irish ladies – Isabel, Marlene, Elaine and Debbie – who were coming over.

I would have kissed all these generous-hearted souls if they'd been in front of me!

'You just don't know what this will mean to us,' I told them over the phone. 'I cannot thank you enough.' And I thanked God for His provision.

As for sorting the line-up, the musician who played the

squeezebox on our single – Phil U, we called him, as we already had a Phil – kindly volunteered his services, as did Tommy and Sarah, our voice coaches. 'I'll stand in for Hannah, as a soloist, and Tommy can stand in for Josh and conduct,' said Sarah.

So, in less than 72 hours, we'd gone from nothing to having accommodation, food, travel and equipment hire all covered – and we had everyone in place for the perform-ance. I felt so blessed. 'It's on!' I whooped down the phone to Phil. 'See you in Manchester.'

What *was* making me anxious, however, was the thought of singing live on national TV. This was to be our very first public appearance as a proper choir – and in front of seven million people. Not only that, but we had to do the new arrangement of the song. I was frightened, I admit. It wasn't that different from the original, but by that point I had so much information in my head that there was almost no room for any more. We couldn't even have a proper rehearsal, because we would only meet the night before, when we all got into Manchester.

But if I was nervous, I did get some sort of reminder – reassurance, almost – about what it was all for. That evening, after the briefest of run-throughs ahead of our early morning start, Phil got out his laptop. 'I've got the finished video for the single,' he said.

Turning all the lights off, we huddled around the com-puter. A hush settled over the room as he pressed play and the familiar music started playing.

'I can't wait to see this,' said Wendy.

There was I, headphones on, in close-up in the darkened studio, singing my solo into the microphone. There was the whole choir in our dark navy T-shirts, emblazoned with the Fishermen's Mission logo. And then other sorts of pictures passed over the screen: Simon, who'd made the video, had carefully worked in photos of the fisherman whom we'd lost. In beautiful watercolour effect, the men we'd loved appeared before us in turn: tired, weather-beaten, smiling. And there was me again, singing the words of my solo part – 'Dance to your daddy / My little laddie' – as Colin appeared, grinning at the camera in a checked shirt and woolly hat on the deck of the *Louisa*; repairing nets in the back garden.

Imagine seeing that for the first time – 'For Those in Peril on the Sea' playing in the background – the faces of your men. There wasn't a dry eye in the house.

'It's perfect,' I said, wiping away a tear. 'I absolutely love it.'

After dinner – courtesy of the hotel – some of the girls were really tired, what with all the travel, a rehearsal and the emotion of watching the music video.

'We've got a 4.30 a.m. start,' I heard people saying as they peeled off for an early night. 'I've got to get some sleep otherwise I'll crack people's TV screens tomorrow!'

Very sensible, I thought – just as Lisa came back from the bar with a tray of piña coladas.

'Come on, ladies,' she cried, 'let's bring a little bit of Essex to Manchester!'

'I like your style,' said Helen with a smile.

'Well, maybe I'll stay a little longer...' I said, sipping my creamy cocktail.

Several cocktails later, I finally wobbled my way to bed.

'Well that's me done, girls, I've got to hit the sack! Night night.'

Really, that evening of laughter was just what I needed. The next morning, my nerves were back in full force – though you wouldn't have guessed how I felt from looking at me.

'Come on, girls – here we go!' I called cheerily, bustling everyone out of the hotel.

Inside, though, I was in turmoil. I only had to sing three or four lines, yes, but mine was the opening solo. I would have done anything to get out of that. I had to hide my jitters, I knew, because the other Fishwives were all looking to me – and they were nervous too.

Even as we were assembled in front of the cameras in the airy studio, ready to be introduced, I could hear the whispering.

'This is mental, isn't it? How come we're on breakfast TV?'

'I was serving fish and chips yesterday!'

'I'm scared,' I muttered to Wendy. 'How many bands do their first proper live performance to seven million people?'

I was terrified; I just wanted to run away. What kept going through my mind was: this was our first live performance ever, and it was front of seven million people.

'Don't think about that – you'll be fine, *we'll* be fine,' she said reassuringly. Wendy, as a professional singer who'd

243

toured with all sorts of people, was our voice of experience. I was so glad to have her standing next to me.

The cameraman signalled to us that there were just minutes to go before we went live.

'I'm so bloody nervous,' said Tracey, one of the Hastings girls. 'I'm wearing two pairs of knickers just in case...'

'Just in case? Just in case of what!' said Toni.

'I've got some Imodium in my bag if that's any use,' offered Didge.

'I don't think anyone's ever crapped themselves on live TV before, have they?' said Toni.

'Well, there was that elephant on *Blue Peter* in the 1970s,' said Barb. 'Where's John Noakes and his zookeeper's broom when you need him?'

Everyone laughed, relieving the tension a little.

But it was time to get serious again, as the seconds ticked away. Waiting under the bright studio lights, I clung to what always sustains me: my faith. 'God has brought us here,' I whispered to myself, 'and He's not going to abandon us now.' He has not brought me here, I thought, with all these women, with all this help, with all this incredible good fortune and goodwill, to abandon us 30 seconds before the camera rolls. It ain't gonna happen! I could forget my lines, that's true. But we're a bunch of housewives, not Madonna. It wouldn't be the end of the world; it's just my pride, my ego, feeling embarrassed that's at stake, nothing more.

So I was just reminding myself how insignificant I was in the grand scheme of things and of the responsibility I felt to the other ladies; and that, no matter how I felt, I was in God's hands.

For somebody who hasn't got a faith, it might seem a load of old nonsense. But, really, I do think that God was guiding us.

Then it was time: the production team counted us in – 'Five, four, three, two, one, and . . . ACTION!'

'Dance to your daddy,' I sang – and soon the rest of the girls were joining in. Yes, I was actually shaking in my shoes as the music played – I'm surprised the camera didn't pick it up – but it was fine. More than fine, in fact. Once my solo was over, I let the moment sink in: we bunch of fishwives were singing live on national TV, and we were sounding good.

Before I knew it, it was over. 'We did it, ladies!' I said, hugging the girls around me, as everyone whooped and cheered with relief that we'd sung it all the way through without any mistakes – not realising the cameras were still rolling! But it didn't matter.

'Well done everyone,' said Phil, clapping. 'That was great – you all did really well.'

Next, Morna, Phil and I had to rush over to a different part of the BBC complex to do an interview for the show. My friend Wendy and Yvonne, another of the gang, were like giggling schoolgirls when the presenter, Bill Turnbull, walked in: 'Oh, Bill, can we have our photos taken?' I must have taken dozens of photos of them together. By now I was totally relaxed: strangely, talking on camera didn't phase me. In contrast, Morna, cool as a cucumber as a singer – she's such a pro – was less of a fan of being grilled on the TV sofa.

But we all rose to the occasion.

'It's such a surprise to us that people are this interested,' I told the presenters. 'We've had such great support and feedback from the press, it's so exciting.'

Next it was Morna's turn.

'We're all related to the fishing industry in some way. My dad was a fisherman who was lost at sea when I was five, but before that, my grandfather and back through the generations, they were all fishermen,' she explained. 'When my dad was lost, there was no body recovered. I think it's really difficult because there's no closure: it's like when someone's missing in action, there's no end point for the family.'

If I could have applauded her as I sat on that sofa, I would have. She was so right.

Soon, we moved on to lighter topics. Can they sing? Phil was asked.

'Yes.' He laughed. 'Yes, yes. They make a lovely noise.' We really were working well as a team, complementing each other's strengths and vulnerabilities.

So quickly, it was all over. Laura, Holly and I then had to do just one more thing: an interview with BBC regional news. It had become a bit of a running joke among us that Laura's clips never made it into the finished version of interviews.

'What's the betting your bit won't make it in?' Holly ribbed Laura – they were old friends.

'Stop it!' said Laura, laughing. 'Surely they won't cut me out of this as well!'

That done, we headed off to Pinewood, the hotel that had laid on a lovely brunch for us – salmon, cold meats, fruit, buck's fizz – to rejoin the rest of the Fishwives.

'Ooh, I feel like a proper celebrity,' said Yvonne. 'Cheers, girls.'

We chinked glasses, to the soundtrack of beeping phones.

'More texts!' squealed Toni, waving hers. 'Loads of them back home just watched us!'

I turned to the Northern Irish ladies. 'You've all come *such* a long way, I'm so glad you're here and you were able to be part of this today.'

Isabel smiled. 'Wouldn't have missed it for the world. We all know the dangers of the sea and we're proud to be doing something for the Mission.'

'It's been a real experience,' said Marlene.

'Don't forget to let us know if you're ever doing anything else like this again,' added Elaine. 'You're not going to get rid of us that easily!'

'I don't ever want to get rid of you!' I said, hugging them all again.

I was on such a high – and, as I sipped my drink, I felt like I could finally take a breath. I'd been so frantic trying to prepare at such short notice: getting all those ladies to Manchester; learning a different version of the song; trying to find funding to pay for us to get there. Throughout, I'd just kept thinking, I'll have my life back after this. Everything will return to normal. Now, having sung our song to millions, I looked around the room, at all the smiling women, and finally thought: my work here is done. Little did I know...

That night I watched the regional news to catch our interviews. Sure enough, only Holly's and mine had made it to the final broadcast.

'Told you,' Laura texted me. 'I'm starting to get a complex now you know!'

I was smiling as I texted her back. What a ride we'd been on!

Fishwives in the Spotlight

'Well, the single's officially out now,' said Lisa. 'Time to put your feet up?' She said it with a smile – she knew I wasn't one to rest on my laurels.

'Well . . .' I said. 'You know, we do keep getting interview requests – our breakfast TV appearance seems to have whetted the appetite.'

That wasn't all that was on my mind.

'With the single available to buy online, I want to get it played everywhere I can,' I told her. 'I've made a big long list of all the radio DJs. I'm going to spend all my spare time phoning everybody up, asking them to play it, and sending them a free promotional copy on CD.'

'All your spare time?' Lisa raised an eyebrow. She knew that was in short supply as it was!

But I was determined. And the regional stations were brilliant, especially those in areas that had a local girl in the choir. They were very supportive. Some played the single, and some arranged interviews. What I desperately wanted was a playlisting: getting played five or six times a day by one radio station, seven days a week. But to achieve that you really have to pay a radio plugger – a professional – thousands to go round all the stations and convince the production teams to pick it up. We didn't have the money to pay someone, and unless you have those relationships yourself it's very unlikely that it will happen.

Nonetheless, we did get some national airplay – from none other than Chris Evans, one of the best-known radio DJs in the country! His producers asked me to do a phone interview with him on his Radio 2 breakfast show before he played the single. As I waited on the phone to be cued into the show, I could feel my heart beating. But Chris was lovely: enthusiastic, supportive. I told him about the choir and my background and my story – how a karaoke-style single had turned into something else – and all the facts about the risks involved in fishing.

'People just aren't aware – I mean, I wasn't, and I was married to a fisherman,' I explained. 'One in 20 fishermen will be seriously injured or lose their lives at work; statistically, it is the most dangerous job in the world in peacetime. What we're doing is trying to raise the profile and let people know the risks that are being taken to put the fish and chips on their plate.'

'It's an extraordinary story, thank you so much for doing this,' Chris said. 'We're more than happy to play it. By the way,' he added, 'it's much better than some old end-of-the-line karaoke single, let me tell you, it's absolutely brilliant.' I liked that!

That appearance just showed me the power of one broadcast. We got so many hits on the Twitter and Facebook accounts I'd set up for the choir – well into the hundreds, after just a 10-minute interview, as people mentioned us in their updates, 'Oh, did you hear that moving story about the Fishwives Choir?' And they were doing more than just talk about us, I realised. We went to number one in the iTunes vocal chart shortly after being on Chris's show.

Because the physical single wasn't in the shops, our iTunes performance – how we were doing in terms of our sales of the single as a download – was a better reflection of our success, rather than the traditional charts. It wasn't for want of trying that we weren't on the shop shelves and into the good old-fashioned Top 40, of course. But it was just not possible, because of the procedure you have to follow to get into the stores – it takes time. Had I known, I would have started the ball rolling much earlier, but I didn't know. That was just one of the lessons I learnt in the process about how the music industry works.

We did make it into the shops in a small way, thanks to the other Fishwives. Lara sold the single from her family's cockle shed, and Lisa was by then running a lovely little shop on the Broadway in Leigh, which also sold copies. The Hastings girls, too, were very proactive and got it into their local Fishermen's Museum. And many of the hard copies went to the Fishermen's Mission, so staff and volunteers could take a box of singles to events, as another way of raising funds.

And then, with no management, no record deal, no financial backing, we were officially named a contender to be a Christmas number one! We had Chris Evans to thank for that. When he'd played our single he'd said, casually, to the listeners, 'Well you know what to do . . . *X Factor*'s there to be beaten!' – referencing the fact that the winner of the TV talent show tended to take the number one spot. And that had sparked articles and chatter in the press; bookies even offered odds on us making number one over the festive period.

'It could be the turn of the Fishwives Choir!' read the breathless release from the Official Charts Company that December. 'The 40-strong group, which is made up of the partners and relatives of fishermen, are releasing their double A-side, "When the Boat Comes In / Eternal Father", to raise money for the Fishermen's Mission. They have the backing of BBC Radio 2's Chris Evans, who was instrumental in the Military Wives' campaign, so watch this space!'

That was all great fun, and scored us and the Mission lots more publicity, even though I knew, realistically, that we wouldn't get the spot: record companies throw thousands at the promotion needed to bag it. But it was such a ride. Up in Edinburgh, our Scottish contingent – Morna, Helen, Yvonne and Sarah – were even treated to lunch by Richard Lochhead, Cabinet Secretary for Rural Affairs and the Environment. He pledged the Scottish government's support of our campaign to raise awareness of the dangers of fishing and the work of the Mission.

Of course, the question people always ask me is, 'How much money have you raised?' And to start with, that was, I thought, the whole point, and I've been waiting with some interest to find out: as I write, it's still not quite clear, as it takes some time for the royalties to come through. 'It will be in four figures,' I'd reply.

But as everything unfolded, I realised something. The benefits to the Mission were so much more than financial. They hadn't had much national press before, but because of the Fishwives the work of the Fishermen's Mission and the purpose of the choir had been talked about across newspapers, regional radio stations, TV. Not only that, but we even did an interview for a mini-documentary with the BBC World Service, where I was able to talk at length about the Fishermen's Mission. So that meant we had achieved international coverage.

Tim from the Mission used to ring me up and say, a smile in his voice, 'What have you started! What have you done!' and every time we were on the radio I'd send him links so he could listen, and in every single interview I always talked about the Fishermen's Mission – I made that a priority. You see, the bigger the profile a charity has, the easier it should be for them to raise funds – meaning that they can carry out more of their charity work.

And, had the charity had to pay for a proper PR company to achieve all that to raise their profile, it could easily have cost them hundreds of thousands of pounds. Just the other day, I saw them on TV talking about how the recent storms had hurt the fishing community badly, in financial terms: they were being turned to as experts on that world; their voice was being heard. I'm not saying that was solely the result of what we did; but after the single came out, I received a letter from the Mission: we were going to receive a special award for promoting the charity. I was really touched. I asked Tim what he made of it all, so here is his explanation of what it meant. 'What we have benefited from – more, really, than the money side of it – is the whole awareness of the Fishermen's Mission and what we do, that we exist. It has been phenomenal. What it has done for us is raise the profile of what we do and why we're here. It's been a huge benefit, but in a different way to what Jane thought.'

There was another unexpected benefit. With the Fish-wives, I'd got really quite used to our mentions in the media; I was always grateful and excited, but it had become part of our lives. But you never think about whose ears your story might have reached – which was brought home to me in February that year, when the Fishwives got a mention in the Houses of Parliament. What was taking place was the second reading of a piece of legislation called the Presump-tion of Death Bill in the House of Lords – meaning that the Members, the great and good, were debating how they wanted to change the law when people go missing. A lady called Baroness Kramer was speaking. The whole point of the Bill was to change the law so that things were no longer needlessly complicated for the families, like mine, she explained.

'The trauma for families and friends when a person goes missing is horrendous,' she said. 'After seven years they can start to take steps to resolve the legal affairs of that person, but without a body they have no death certificate, and without a death certificate a person is legally assumed to be alive.' Well, that sounded very familiar. As she went on, there were steps that relatives could take, but 'you really could not invent a more bureaucratic and stressful system . . . The families and associates of missing people are often left in an intolerable limbo well before the seven-year mark is reached.'

And then she mentioned me. 'A number of people will have seen the quotes from Jane Dolby, who has created the Fishwives Choir, on the pattern of the Military Wives Choir, following the death of her husband at sea. It was eight months before his body was found. During that period his wife could not get a death certificate and therefore could not access his bank account or claim benefits. She was left without an income and the Fishermen's Mission gave her and her children emergency financial support to enable them, essentially, to survive. She has dedicated the first of the albums by the Fishwives Choir to the Fishermen's Mission, but it illustrates the problems that so many people face.'

I was so pleased that, in some small way, my ordeal might help to prevent other people's burdens from being made heavier when they were at their lowest. And I was even more pleased when I learnt that the Bill was voted through by both the House of Commons and the House of Lords to become an Act of Parliament – meaning it is now part of our law. I sincerely hope this means that no one ever has to go through what I and others went through.

Charting Our Journey

'Are you like a female version of the Fishermen's Friends?' said a man's voice down the phone. 'I'd like to make an enquiry about booking you for the opening of a fish and chip shop.'

'Oh!' I said. 'Have you heard us sing then?'

'Well, no. But I've heard *of* you.'

And somehow this chap had the impression that we were like the Fishermen's Friends, the shanty singers from Port Isaac on Cornwall's coast. They'd been going strong for years, made up of fishermen, lifeboat men and coastguards past and present. I knew that the 10 or so of them sounded fabulous, a real wall of sound.

'I'm so sorry,' I said, 'we really can't accept your offer' – just as I turned down every invitation to perform that was coming in.

And there were a surprising number of them. The choir was never set up to be anything other than a one-off charity release. Throughout, as much as I loved the experience, I kept saying to friends and family, 'Oh, it will be good when this is all over, I can't wait to get my life back.' It was so all-consuming, you see. I was juggling a 30-hour-a-week job, being an only parent, and all of this. I was dropping balls everywhere, only they weren't the Fishwives' balls, they were everyone else's! I hadn't considered that people would want us to perform.

Other people thought differently. All the publicity around the single had triggered something. I had started getting loads of phone calls and emails asking us to perform: could you come and play at this beer festival, or this shanty-themed event? Reluctantly, I'd have to decline: 'Thank you so much for inviting us, I'm afraid it's just impossible. There's more than three dozen of us, only one song, and we're spread all over the UK.'

Still, the enquiries kept coming in. I said no to everybody. Some people were a bit funny about it; they didn't understand that I couldn't get 40 women – who had only learnt one song – from all over the country together to come and sing at the opening of a supermarket, and not even have their fares covered. I couldn't afford to get everybody there, let alone to meet for rehearsals in advance. We just couldn't do it.

'But I thought you were a charity choir,' was the inevitable refrain.

'Well, yes, we are,' I'd explain, 'but we haven't got the money.'

Still, there must be a way of making it work, I'd tell myself. For, as much as it had consumed my life, I didn't want it to stop, being part of the choir was such great fun. It would be such a shame to lose momentum.

'It's so nice to hear some real music,' people would tell me – mums in the playground, friendly faces on the streets of Leigh. 'It's so nice to have just normal people who like singing represented. Good on you!'

The British really support the underdog, and we were such an unlikely success story. The other thing, of course, that had happened in the process was that my love of singing had been reawakened. I'd done all this for the Mission, and for Colin, but in return I'd received my own priceless gift. I'd never expected that singing would be in my life again, and now here it was, heart and centre. That was really wonderful.

So I wanted to carry on, but how? In my head we were a complete unit: what people had seen on telly – and I thought that is what they'd want. It didn't cross my mind that I could offer an alternative. But then that call from the man with the chippie, mentioning the male shanty group, got my brain whirring. Hold on, I thought, there is a way I can do this, if I can just make the logistics work: a smaller group, members who can make regular rehearsals, some way of covering our expenses – excitement stole over me.

'This is the plan going forward,' went my email to the Fishwives. 'We have had a lot of performance requests and if we are going to do this, the only way is to make it a commercially viable concern, where – even if we don't take a fee – at least our expenses are covered, so nobody will be out of pocket. But,' I added, 'it will require weekly rehearsals.'

I didn't want anybody to feel left out so I offered everyone the opportunity to carry on if they wanted to. After all, I didn't know their individual circumstances. For all I knew, one of them could have been a secret billionaire and quite happy to fly down once a week! But although everyone wished us loads of luck, most said they couldn't commit on an ongoing basis, explaining that they had jobs, families – it was just impossible. And I quite understood that what was practical as a one-off effort was quite different as a standing date.

Although I must say that they were never short on commitment. One Fishwife, Helen, had actually gone and got our name and logo as a tattoo! People had already given up a week of their time to recording, as well as time for photo shoots, interviews with their local press, the lot. For many people their commitment to the choir had been for the Mission; carrying on doing it for fun wasn't what they were in it for. Putting a half-hour set together, I knew, would mean months and months of rehearsing – especially for people like us, who aren't professionals.

So we made the decision among a few of us local girls that we would take it forward: Lee, Laura, Lara and I, as well as Wendy, my friend the professional singer, who'd sung at my wedding all those years before. For Lisa, sadly, it was no longer possible to continue. She ran her own business, had a small son and was just not able to commit in the way she knew she needed to. 'I just can't do it any more, Jane, I'm really sorry.'

'Don't apologise, Lisa.' I gave her a squeeze. 'I completely get it. You've already stuck at this for almost two years – and we've been lucky to have you for so long.' We'd been friends for the best part of 20 years and nothing would change that.

I was thrilled, though, that Tommy, one of our two vocal coaches, said she'd like to stay involved; Morna from Scotland was keen; likewise Tommy, who was also not from the area and was the only one without a connection to fishing when she'd got involved. But she'd given so much of her time, and she was a great vocalist. So the Fishwives in its new incarnation became Tommy, Morna, Wendy, myself and the 'three Ls' – Laura, Lara and Lee – on backing vocals. I got some boys involved: my son Josh on the keyboards; roped in Rob, a local guitar player; Phil U, who'd already played the squeezebox for us; and a couple of newbies – John or Russ – on bass, depending on who was available.

And, from the start, it worked: Morna lived miles away, but I would just send her the MP3 file of our recorded rehearsal and she'd learn it long-distance; other people wouldn't be able to do that. I'd say, 'Could you take the top harmony,' and that would be it. Tommy too, being so experienced, could just pick things up.

But on a personal level I wasn't finding it quite such smooth sailing. After months of being so busy, I was fast reaching the end of my capacity to keep all the balls in the air. One evening, as we packed away our gear after a rehearsal, I was surprised to find myself near to tears.

'I'm not sure how much longer I can do this,' I admitted to the group. 'I feel so stressed with work, the kids, all the Fishwives stuff and I'm not coping very well. I'm so worried a lot of the time and my mind is constantly churning things over, so I can't sleep properly either.'

'Right-o, missus,' said Lee. 'Your problem, if you don't mind me saying, is that you are a bit of a control freak and not very good at delegating. We are all here watching you get worn to a frazzle and all happy to help – but you have just got to let us.'

'She's right,' said Lara, 'we're all in this together, you know.'

'Jane,' said Rob, 'from now on, leave the musical direction to me. I know what I'm doing, you don't have to manage it all on your own. If you don't like what we are doing you can always tell us, but that's a responsibility I'm happy to take off your shoulders.'

'And if it's any help,' added Phil, 'I can set up an online gig calendar so you don't have to keep texting and emailing everyone about dates.'

I was really touched.

'Now, what about the money?' asked Lee. 'Some of these gigs coming up are paying our expenses and the finances all need to be managed properly.'

'Oh God, that's a boring job.' I pulled a face.

Laura put her hand up. 'Er, hello! Have we been introduced? My name's Laura and I *love* admin!' It was true, we all knew she was super-organised – after all, she was an office manager in her day-to-day life. 'I also love a spreadsheet so I'll volunteer for that job!'

'And I'll help with the money,' offered Lee. 'Me and Laura will be the treasurers and deal with all that side of things, but' – she cocked a thumb towards Laura – 'she can do the spreadsheets, seeing as she likes them so much.'

'Thank you, you bloody lovely lot!' I smiled, blinking away my tears.

And they were as good as their word. During the next rehearsal, Laura handed out folders.

'Right, everyone,' she said with authority. 'In your folders are printouts of all the lyrics, the gig dates and a calendar for us to pencil in forthcoming rehearsal dates.'

'Blimey,' said Lara, flicking through a sheaf of A4. 'You really do like admin, don't you?'

Things kept falling into place. After that night in the Hastings pub had piqued my interest, I'd thought a lot about sea shanties. That evening singalong had been gobsmacking for me: how the musical heritage was still the lifeblood of the community. It was just coursing through its people's veins; everyone knew these songs. But I realised from my own experience that that part of the fishing culture had been lost in many coastal regions.

A shanty, of course, is a song sung on a boat – they are songs to work to. But as I immersed myself in learning more about them, I started to realise their fuller significance. The men would sing these shanties, never knowing if they'd come back to shore. They sang to keep their morale up – it was music to keep you alive. That was something I also knew about: that was, really, what the Fishwives and our music had done for me, with our own take on an old sea shanty. In this folk music, I was utterly sure, lay our path forward. I wanted to make the shanties much more accessible to the younger generation, to stop them dying out. To modernise them, too – not to take anything away from their traditional beauty or their messages, but I thought there was room to give them a different treatment, just as we'd done with our single.

So I started writing songs, as I've always loved to do, even if nobody ever heard them. And the inspiration just flowed. One song told how X marks the spot – both the elusive reward that takes our loved ones away from us, and the X on the calendar that women use to count down the days till their men's return. 'Stormy old days / Out on the waves / Families waiting ashore,' I'd sing, trying different chords on my guitar. 'Braving the cold / May your anchor hold / And seas bring you all home once more.' Another, 'Drunken Sailor' – a play on the traditional shanty of the same name – was written from the perspective of the woman who was waiting for her man to come home. 'My sailor man's coming back to me / He's gonna be like a bear with a sore head,' it went. 'Back in the heart of his family / You'd better hope he's made some changes.' Happily, that wasn't autobiographical!

The ideas just kept coming. One very dear to my heart, 'Jessie', took inspiration from the selkie myth. Selkies are magical beings: creatures that look like seals but, if they remove their skins, are revealed as beautiful people. As the story goes, sometimes a fisherman would catch a selkie as she came on the beach to run about without her skin, to make a lovely bride. He'd hide her skin, so she couldn't return to the water and sometimes his selkie wife would be happy with her married life and family, and sometimes she'd pine for her home under the waves. The myth seemed to embody the pulls that we constantly face as women, torn between our different responsibilities and longings.

I felt I had so much to communicate about this world of mine, which could also express the trials and heartbreak everyone fears. At the same time, I'd started bouncing my rough ideas for melodies and lyrics off Phil and his right-hand man Robin, who'd played some guitar on the original single. Over the phone, emailing each other snippets of music, we'd work together as co-writers, honing and developing the songs.

I started to think about a next step: recording an album. Aside from showcasing this new music, there were other reasons. In our new guise, we had to find a way to become commercially viable, I knew. If we can make a CD and sell copies at gigs, that could generate some income for us, I thought – just to squirrel away some funds so that if we were asked to play, say, a festival in Devon, we wouldn't have to say to the organisers, 'Well, not unless you give us £500 for petrol to get us all there!' We were happy to perform for nothing, but none of us could afford to actually end up out of pocket as a result. Also, an album would give us an identifiable sound: show people who knew us from the single that we were not just choral. We could send it out to organisers to get some bookings for next year, so it would work as a promotional tool as well as a bit of an earner.

But what, in the end, convinced me that I was on the right path had nothing to do with the practicalities at all. I'd sat down at my computer to pull together a list of our media coverage, when I found something else. Searching online for references to us, I stumbled across mentions of other fishwives choirs. What was this? My jaw dropped as I read on. Fishwives choirs were nothing new, I discovered. In days gone by they'd thrived in certain coastal towns, becoming well-known fixtures in places like Edinburgh's Newhaven area and Fisherrow, also up in Scotland. Judging from the brown-tinged photos posted online, the members looked as if they had ranged from three years old to about 83.

I kept reading. There were others too: I learnt about the herring girls, who used to follow their fishermen around the coast, singing while they worked. Every autumn these hordes of Scotswomen would leave their families and travel along the British coastline following the fishing fleet. Working in teams of three, they'd gut the herrings the men caught and pack them into barrels, layered with salt, to preserve the fish. It was tough work, often carried out in the open air, and went on well into winter. Sometimes the women would actually faint with the cold. Separated from their loved ones, toiling hard to survive, they'd keep their spirits up by singing hymns and folk songs. It seemed the tradition went on for the best part of a century before the herring boom came to an end after the Second World War. Again, the role music played in these women's lives just spoke to my experiences, and those of the other Fishwives.

Suddenly, I felt so very connected to a part of our culture that I hadn't even known had existed. I was so excited I had to call someone. 'Blimey, Wendy,' I told her. 'We didn't even know it, but we've been resurrecting a piece of our heritage!'

It was so fitting: I'd been talking in my interviews to promote the choir about how women's voices are not often heard from the fishing community – and now, I found, they used to be, at least in this way. It was clear to me what we should do with the choir.

'I know what we should do now,' I said, rushing out my words. 'We'll sing shanties – but shanties that are relevant to the modern generation, and from a woman's perspective.' We'd take up the baton from the fishwives' choirs of days gone by and keep alive something that we'd almost lost: the musical heritage of our last hunter-gatherer tradition.

I knew that Colin would have backed me completely. He was never someone to shout about what he was doing, but he loved the world that he belonged to – it was so utterly key to the man he was. This would have been right up his street.

From that point onwards, something seemed to click. 'I'm loving all these new song ideas you're sending,' said Phil on the phone one day. 'Now, can you take some time to come to my studio and we'll start recording them?' So, over the next few weeks I would do the school run, take the train to London and record with Phil and Robin all day, then rush home to collect the kids and do homework, tea and bedtimes. Eventually, with their input, my half-written songs became fully fledged compositions – and I started to think more and more about how we could make them into a proper album.

Riding the Wave

'Come on, girls,' I whispered, away from the mic. 'This is it.' Standing under the stage lights, I looked back out over the hot, dark hall. As the organiser carried out her introductions, explaining the Fishwives' story, I could see even in the gloom that it was standing room only at the back.

Earlier, as we'd been warming up backstage, we'd been told that the line of people queuing for a spot in our performance stretched out of the door, right down the stairs to the foyer below. We were a bit of a curiosity, I knew, this bunch of local ladies who had been on the telly, been in the press – but nobody had actually heard us sing in person! This was our chance to show everybody what we could do.

It felt so right that this was where the Fishwives would make their first performance in front of a live audience – in my home town. What could be more fitting, either, than making our debut at a festival focused on the sea? There were speakers and exhibitions and performers – and us. More than anything else, though, the date had confirmed it for me. Five years ago today, 10 November, I'd lost Colin. To go from tears to song felt the perfect way to mark that terrible anniversary. I still desperately miss him, I thought, yet here I am, standing on a stage with good friends, about to sing – maybe with cracked voices, that's true, but also with great pride in the men we've lost, and in the men who still risk their lives at sea.

I scanned the crowd again, my nerves mounting. There were friends and neighbours: Lisa and a lot of other colleagues-turned-friends had come to support us, I noticed. Then I spotted another familiar face in the crowd: Lesley, one of the ladies from the widows' support group online that had been such a lifeline for me. She lived in Essex, but a distance away, saw the event advertised on Facebook and travelled down. You've come a long way on your own, I thought. That's really sweet.

Still, there were more faces that I didn't recognise. My stomach turned over again. Yes, we'd performed as the Fishwives on national TV, but this felt very different. My stage fright still hadn't gone away. I knew that I could talk a good talk and get publicity for things, but I remained very self-conscious. More than that, I was frightened – the stage will never be my comfort zone.

But what's very different about doing this, I told myself, as opposed to that band back in my twenties, is that this is bigger – and that's nothing to be scared of. So much of how you cope with things is to do with motivation. Back then, it was about us wanting to be rock stars, to be famous; until, of course, I set foot on stage for the first time and realised that was absolutely not what I wanted at all, that the idea of everybody looking at me was absolutely terrifying.

This time around, it isn't about me. This project has

always been about Colin and the other men, highlighting the dangers of fishing, raising awareness of the Fishermen's Mission, I thought. I took a deep breath, and breathed out. When I removed my ego from something, I found, it was less terrifying; it was less about me. So although I was still scared – I really was! – it wasn't the same debilitating fear that I had in times before.

And I wasn't alone, I reassured myself. I had Wendy to my left, and Lee, Lara and Laura to my right. As we stood there, exchanging glances while the lady explained who we were, I gave them a smile. I'd set foot on a stage before; the three of them had never done anything like this in their lives! They were housewives with normal jobs, Laura an office manager, Lara a hairdresser and helping out at the family cockle shed, and Lee a nurse. This was a completely new world for them – and I was completely sure that they could do it. In the last six months they'd been on the radio, on TV, in the national press, giving interviews to promote our cause. They'd gone from timid and tongue-tied to really experienced and confident. It was incredible to witness their transformation.

'Ladies and gentlemen, I give you the Fishwives Choir!' As the organiser walked off the stage, the band started up.

We'd agreed we couldn't perform our single with just five of us – this big choral thing, with four solo parts – as it would have meant having one person trying to do all the chorus in the background. So we'd prepared two new songs, rehearsing in our new formation. We opened with 'Ocean Bound', the lyrics of which were very personal to me:

Song of the Sea

Oh I wish that my love was
a caribou,
that he was bound to ground
earth to foot.

I wish that my love was
a bird on high
flying safely
in the sky.

But my love is ocean bound
water may pull him down
and though my heart cries out
my love is ocean bound.

I long for my love to be
close to home,
that he was in my arms
no sea to roam.

But the salt, the swell, the pull
will always be
in the hearts and souls
of those at sea.

But my love was ocean bound
Water has pulled him down
And though my heart cried out
My love was ocean bound.

It was a mournful melody, and the room was still as we sang – people were really listening. After that, we had deliberately decided to end on a more raucous, foot-stomping note. It was time for our 'Drunken Sailor'. That got them going! We left the stage to a storm of applause. It was such a thrill, everyone congratulating us afterwards. I was relieved, and proud of our little unit.

In the following days, I put a video of our festival performance on YouTube and more invitations to perform came in – and this time I could accept them. (Although it did make me laugh: every time we were asked to play, people would say, 'Oh could you just do a couple of songs?' I'd think, thank God, we still only know a couple of songs.) We got loads of bookings for festivals over the coming summer; we were even invited to perform at the National Maritime Museum in Greenwich.

Meanwhile, in typical flying-by-the-seat-of-my-pants style, I booked a recording session for an album. No, I didn't know how I was going to pay for it, but I was sure it would work out. I wasn't worried – I just knew that I was doing the right thing, just knew that I would be able to raise the money. We'll find it, I thought, something will happen.

But when we tried crowdfunding again, we didn't reach anywhere near our target to cover the recording and have the album made into a CD. The problem was, there was only a limited pool of friends and family to turn to. Some people had been very generous, but it just wasn't appropriate to keep asking.

At one point I said to the other girls, 'I can't do this on my own.'

Lee, very candidly, admitted that she was reluctant to go down this route again. 'I pushed it with the single, I asked people for help – and I'm really sorry, but I just don't want to keep asking my friends, it doesn't feel right.'

'I completely understand,' I said. 'I feel the same.'

So Laura had this brilliant idea of doing a fundraising quiz night, which got us part of the way.

Then, one day, I got an email from a chap called Colin. He was from the Fishmongers Company, he said, and would I like to come and meet him to discuss a few things? I looked online and saw that the address on his email was next to Billingsgate, the huge fish market by Canary Wharf in London. A few days later, as we'd arranged, I caught the train to London to meet this fishmonger. But once I arrived at the market, deserted after the early morning rush when all the chefs and the rest go and buy their stock, I phoned him on my mobile.

'I'm here,' I said, 'but the market's empty – where do I go?'

'Oh no,' he replied. 'You're in the wrong building,' and he directed me to an address nearby.

My jaw dropped as I walked through the door. This was a building that could only be described as palatial, decked out in plum and bottle-green. It was so unexpected – like a stately home. Bloody hell, I thought, I was expecting to meet a man behind a fish stall! Colin came down and met me and explained. I was standing in the Fishmongers'

Hall, a Grade I listed building on the north bank of the Thames. The dining room alone could hold 200 people. As for this Fishmongers Company – full name, the Worshipful Company of Fishmongers – it was one of the 12 great livery companies of the City of London, organisations which had their roots in the different trades, fish included. King Edward I had granted the Company's first charter in about 1272, which meant that no fish could be sold in London except by the 'Mystery of Fishmongers'.

That was a long time ago, of course, and though the Company was still very involved with the fishing world, I was more likely to find Colin (a major general after years in the army) and his colleagues overseeing philanthropic work than flogging Dove sole. In fact, I realised, some of the money the Fishermen's Mission gave to us in grants and help had probably originated from the Company, which funds relevant fishing-related organisations.

'We'd like to support you,' said Colin, and asked if the choir would perform at something called the Lady Fish lunch, a do for ladies involved with the Company, the wives of various dignitaries. 'Of course,' I said, 'we'd love to,' and over the following weeks we planned our return.

Well, this was pretty different to our last gig; the ladies were all very refined and reminded me of Camilla Parker-Bowles! At one point I spotted one of the table plans: some seemed to have a title. But they were lovely to us, terribly interested in what we were up to.

'The choir was set up by Jane following the death of her husband,' Colin explained to them, 'and, ladies, I would like you to return home and use your wifely influences with your husbands and ask them to approve the Fishwives' application to the Company.'

He was great, completely on our side. But there was one funny moment. As we were doing our sound check, the bass player I'd recruited was moving a few things around, just getting set up, when a nice older man came up to him.

'I say, old chap,' he told him, 'would you mind being careful with that picture? It's worth a small fortune.' It was like another world.

After we performed, we were taken downstairs to a beautiful library where a lovely lunch had been laid on for us and Colin came and spoke to us again.

'I'm cautiously optimistic. I think you went down very well; the ladies liked your story.' He went on: 'Perhaps you should set up as a charity.'

While this potential grant might work as a one-off, it would be tricky to support an organisation that didn't have charitable status, he explained.

'I really don't want to,' I told him. 'Look, I work for a charity. I know how hard it is to get the funding in. I've been fundraising for the Fishwives and it's a really difficult job. You have to have a board of trustees. How will we ever earn any money to cover our costs? I'm really sorry, Colin,' I said, 'but it's not something I'm interested in.'

'Before you say no,' he said, 'let me tell you the benefits.' And then he did – how it could make fundraising easier, and that being not-for-profit didn't have to mean that nobody gets paid or has to cover their expenses. That was the gist of it. Our band, in the room while we were having this conversation, saw the benefits before I did, and started to chime in too.

It was as if a light went on in my head. It dawned on me that I could marry my two worlds – my youth work and the maritime world – by using the Fishwives to raise money for related causes: perhaps funding places for young offenders on sailing trips that taught them how to behave in a different, better way. And what about people like my kids, who'd been bereaved by the sea? How brilliant would it be if we could say, 'We'll pay for a family who've had a terrible time to have a break.' Suddenly, I was really excited about all the opportunities that becoming a charity might bring. And that's why, as a I write, a year after we were raising money for charity, we're now in the throes of becoming one – we're in the process of applying for charitable status. Not only that, but those fish ladies totally came through for us Fishwives: we got the grant to fund our six-track album.

Over the Horizon

By Christmas, we had a handful of performances under our belt. We'd only been singing our two songs each time, but they'd taken months of preparation to get right. Now, with a summer of gigs quickly approaching, my sessions with Phil and Robin meant we had enough new music to stage a proper set – but we also had to get the songs sounding good. I was feeling the pressure.

'It must be bloody agony for you, Wendy,' I said as we finished a session one evening. 'Hope you know how grateful I am.'

As such an experienced singer, Wendy had nailed her parts at the first rehearsal, but she was so committed that she turned up week after week so the rest of us could get ours down pat.

'Don't be silly,' she said firmly. 'I *like* being here.'

'The problem is,' explained Lee, 'I learn my bits at home and I can remember them perfectly, but then when I get to rehearsals and stand next to anyone singing a different harmony to mine, my own melody goes clean out of my head. I end up singing whatever the person next to me is singing. I'm so frustrated with myself.'

'I feel the same – and I'm losing confidence,' I admitted.

'Listen,' said Phil U. 'I mainly play on the folk circuit and we have a very different set of expectations that are not solely about hitting the right notes at the right time. So what if you forget a harmony? So what if you come in a little bit late? Don't make it all such hard work that you forget to have fun, and forget to allow the audience to have fun, too. I'm telling you, we've been stuck in this rehearsal room for weeks and weeks and the way that we will get much better is by going out, getting on stage and gigging.'

'But we're nowhere near ready,' I said, alarmed.

'He's right, Jane,' said Rob, our guitar player. 'I've been in plenty of bands and there's no substitute for doing it live. It really does pull you together in a way that no rehearsal can.'

'But none of us want to go on stage and look stupid,' said Lara, 'I want to get it right before we play live.'

'We'll get it as good as we can,' said Phil, 'but we've got to stop comparing the act to the bands you see on TV. We're a folk act and folk is a bit different. It's about heart, community, storytelling – and we are part of that tradition.' He spoke with such conviction.

I looked him in the eye. 'You really believe we can pull it off then, Phil?'

'Absolutely. And you can't forget that most of you have never done this before. I think you're all doing an incredible job. It takes guts to walk out on stage and I admire you girls for it. You need courage to try something as exposing as this.'

'Well, I feel like I'd rather expose any bit of my body rather my voice, quite frankly!' said Lara.

'I don't think it'll be that sort of gig,' I said, laughing.

'Look, Laura and Lee, why don't you both sing the same parts in future and stand next to each other,' suggested Rob. 'Then, if you do end up singing what the person next to you sings you'll be absolutely right! Let's give it a go now.'

So, Lee and Laura tried out the idea – and it worked perfectly.

We turned a corner that night. It may have taken us months to learn our first two songs, but after that it was like the penny had dropped. From that moment on, adding songs to our set became a much faster process. We were all rooting for each other and spurring each other on, lifting each other when one of us was low, or losing impetus or confidence. The Fishwives was so much more than a musical group to all of us. It offered a safe environment in which to grow, to be encouraged and to encourage. Once again I was reminded that I was part of something extremely special.

We planned to record the album locally, in Chelmsford, Essex. We had Wendy and the three Ls, Morna and Yvonne coming down from Scotland – and even Esther, yes, our maritime academic, was joining us again for an appearance! It was going to be much tougher than recording the single during that week in Hastings, though, I knew.

In the run-up, Phil Da Costa, producing again, had his work really cut out with six songs on the album. He worked like a dog, for weeks, preparing all the tracks in advance. I was so lucky he wanted to stay involved. By this point, it felt as if we'd just automatically fallen into different roles, covering all the bases needed to release a piece of music. He took care of the technical side, all the stuff that I didn't know about, and I would take on the press, the promotion, the organising. We planned to keep the single on the album too, so there would still be a charitable element, with a share of the sales going to the Fishermen's Mission.

But we got there, got ready, and so, a year to the day that we'd started recording our single, I found myself back in the studio, this time laying down tracks for our album. I could feel my face breaking into a huge grin as I saw Morna, Yvonne and Esther again.

'Hello, hello, we've missed you!'

'You too, oh come here, give us a hug.'

'Love your hair, that new style really suits you' – it was a flurry of kisses and greetings. It felt so good being in the other girls' company once again, and even better to be in the studio. 'What's the master plan then with this CD?' asked Yvonne. 'Is it another fundraiser?'

'Well,' I explained, 'I am going to give lots of copies to the Fishermen's Mission to sell, so they can keep whatever money they make from those sales, but essentially we are just hoping we might get a bit of radio airplay and perhaps sell a few at gigs to cover our costs.'

Phil chipped in. 'Primarily, it's a promotional item to showcase the new songs that you're doing.'

'Ah, but once Richard Branson hears it, there'll be no stopping us,' said Yvonne, smiling.

'Yeah!' I replied. 'Wouldn't that be good?'

The week went by in a blur; it was hard work, but musically so fulfilling. As well as our usual band musicians, we had an incredible mandolin player called Joe. He brought the tracks to life in a way that almost made me cry. Who would ever have thought those ideas that I sang into my phone and sent to Phil could sound so lovely? All too soon, it was over – but I had a summer of gigs to look forward to. I couldn't wait.

For our first proper season of performances, we'd been booked to play at the Dorset Seafood Festival, the Newlyn Fish Festival, the Bexhill Festival of the Sea, the Royal Greenwich Tall Ships Festival, Fishstock in Brixham and the Newquay Fish Festival. We even had a booking from the seafood chef Rick Stein for the famous Padstow Christmas event. There were also a couple of private functions, too.

Dorset was our first big show. Weymouth harbour, where it was held, was rammed with visitors as the sun beat down.

'Oh my good God, look at all those people!' I breathed. 'I think I've forgotten all the words.'

But as we sang the crowd cheered – and clapped for more as we came to an end.

'Thank you, thank you so much,' I said down the mic. 'We've got some CDs for sale for a fiver if you want to come and see us afterwards.'

Quickly, Laura and Lee served the small queue which

had formed at the side of the stage, while Tommy did her best impression of a market trader.

'Fishwives CDs!' she shouted. 'Come and get them!'

Catching my eye, she dropped her voice: 'I think I'm starting to enjoy this you know...'

'You boys were right about the live gigs getting us tighter on stage,' I said to Phil U and Rob.

'Yep,' said Phil, 'we are definitely getting better.'

That summer of shows, we rose to the challenge of balancing work with weekend gigs and childcare. It wasn't always easy – but it was fun. Towards the end of the season we had a final weekend of gigs: Brixham and Newquay.

'This all seemed like a really good idea when we were booking them all in,' I groaned, climbing into the minibus we'd hired to take us to Brixham at 6 a.m.

'I know what you mean,' said Lee with a yawn. 'I have to work so many shifts to be able to get time off to do all this. I'm worn out.'

'I must admit it's a bloody long drive for a bunch of old crocs like us,' I said.

'Oi! Speak for yourselves in the back there!' said Laura from the driving seat. She was only 28.

But as we approached the Devon coast, our spirits lifted.

'Look at that view,' said Lee, 'it's breathtaking.'

'Where are we staying again, Jane?' said Rob.

'Wait and see,' I told him. 'You'll love it.'

We were staying on the most beautiful old sailing trawler called the *Pilgrim of Brixham* that a charity had kindly lent us for the weekend. The only thing was, the *Pilgrim* was moored on the outside of two other boats, which meant we had to clamber over the other vessels – with all our bags – to get aboard.

'I'm going to fall in that gap!' I peered over the edge. 'It looks like quite a leap . . . I'm hardly a slip of a thing.'

And sure enough, when my turn came, I could feel the wood start to shift under me.

'Oh dear!' I cried. 'It's moving, help!'

As the men pulled the side ropes to bring the boat in closer, I plopped over the side – and was finally aboard. The sky over the busy fishing town of Brixham was an amazing pink. We all just stood silently, each of us taking in the view.

But the evening turned to comedy once again. Climbing into bed – bunks lining the sides of the boat – I could hardly speak for laughing. 'I'm bloody stuck, give us a push!' Tommy and Lee tried to shove me in the bunk. 'I'm not very flexible.'

'Ah, Jane,' said Rob from his bunk. 'Speaking of flexible, I'm going to go on deck in the morning and do some yoga as the sun's coming up. If you fancy joining me, just bring a couple of cushions.'

'I'll definitely do it with you, Rob,' said Tommy.

I didn't want to commit myself. 'Hmm, I'll see what I feel like in the morning.'

Still, early the next day, I joined Tommy and Rob on deck. Phil was already awake, playing his accordion towards the bow of the boat.

'Panting first,' said Rob, 'breathe in and exhale fast and hard.'

Dutifully, we followed his instructions.

'Gentle stretches next,' said Rob. 'On your backs, legs in the air, ladies.'

At that point I caught sight of two old fishermen on the boat next to us – so close we could have had a conversation.

'Look at that lot,' said one to the other. 'I don't know what sort of band they are but they look like a right bunch of weirdos to me.' I started to giggle again. It was one of those weekends when you hardly catch your breath, you're laughing so hard. It was such a joyful end to a wonderful summer.

Really, that takes us to where we – I – am currently: back to our normal lives. But those normal lives are different these days. Just look at where we all are now.

As Lee said to me the other day, 'Doing this has been the single most empowering thing I've done in my life.' She's been having singing lessons, bought a microphone, even taking the lead vocal on some of our songs. Singing, she says, has opened up a door within her that she never even knew was there; and whatever happens, she's going to carry on.

Laura says the same thing: that the Fishwives has brought so much to her life; that she goes to work with a spring in her step; that she's just part of something that makes her so happy. As she puts it, 'I was always my husband's wife, or my son's mum. So I needed something that I could do for me – and this just filled it completely. And if I've got a problem, or something's happened, I always end up telling the Fishwives, because they're really supportive. It's having this other group of girls who are there for you.'

Indeed, speak to any of our Fishwives, these women who've brought so much to my life, and I think they'll say they same: in giving – our time, our effort, our voices – each one of us has gained so much more.

Once a Fishwife, always a Fishwife, of course. Already, I've every intention that when we're singing at festivals, events, those ladies based up and down the country can come and join us again, catch up for a good sing-along. For even those who aren't in a position to carry on singing regularly have carried on with what matters even more, the friendship, messaging each other, keeping up with what other people are doing. As Sue says, 'I think we'll always be friends, even though we're a long way away.'

As for me, I'm looking ahead to the future. As well as the album, we've more gigs planned, rehearsals to attend, more songs to work on. As I hoped, we've a shanty night planned in Leigh, just like the one we loved while we were recording in Hastings.

We've even had the opportunity to appear on a TV talent show – one of the big ones. I was very tempted at first – I said an almost definite yes. Until Henry said, 'Hold on: have you really thought about this? Do you want to be telling your story with sad music and pictures of Colin in the background?' I couldn't help but feel Henry was right: I wanted Colin to be more than a television backstory. When I mentioned what was on my mind to the rest of the Fishwives, they backed me up. 'We completely agree,' they said. 'We had our reservations. We would have gone along with it, but we don't think it's the right platform either.' I was so relieved. Everybody was in agreement that it was the perfect show for some people – but maybe not for us.

I felt even more sure that we'd done the right thing when we received offers for other shows that felt a much better fit for us. There's a Radio 4 documentary about us in the works too, and all sorts of opportunities. We're really excited.

And as we keep getting busier, Laura and Lee are still helping me keep the show on the road. There's so much to do, what with organising everything, co-ordinating the press, keeping our website updated. So those two have taken over dealing with all the money and the admin, looking after the transport, the practical things. Perhaps that's just as well! Recently I discovered the dictation app on my iPhone. I was thrilled – I could just dictate all the emails I needed to send. Stuck in traffic, I'd instruct the phone to email whomever. Still, while I thought I was being efficient, that did mean I couldn't check what I was sending from behind the wheel – off it went. So, one busy day, writing to confirm our booking with Rick Stein for the festival he runs, I managed to email his PA asking for expenses towards 'coke and travel'. I meant *cost* and travel, needless to say. I also told the Maritime Museum in Greenwich that we could offer 'full sex' with audience participation – rather than 'a full set'. So Laura's and Lee's efficiency and help have been much appreciated!

I'm still in touch with Tim Jenkins – for me, he's the

face of the Fishermen's Mission – at least once a week by phone, or text, or Facebook. Sometimes I do say to him, 'I don't know if I can manage it – I feel like it's too much, I'm really stressed.' And we might pray together down the phone: 'Please God, give me wisdom in handling this, please bring the right people to me, let me make wise decisions, keep me humble.' Tim tells me: 'We feel really blessed that you're our friend, that you're doing this for the Mission.' That means a lot.

It's a roller coaster still, and I love it. We've created something magical, bigger than us, I think to myself. Indeed, that's what went through my mind, that final day in the studio, as I looked around at these friends, both old and new, crowded into the little room. What a wonderful week of fun, friendship, making music. From the depths of tragedy, we've risen to celebrate hope and joy.

For all that you've brought me, I thank you, Colin.

Epilogue

There was a time when I honestly thought that I would never smile again. I remember, that first summer after Colin died, with the sun shining and the skies blue, feeling dead inside. How could I ever be happy when this man whom I loved with all my heart – and I would always love – had gone? How could I ever be happy again? I thought I would never recover, never smile again, certainly never sing again; that I would be destined for ever just to go through the motions of life.

To anybody who is reading this, if perhaps what I say strikes a chord with you, I want to offer you hope. It is always darkest just before the dawn.

Today, I can't wait for the summer to arrive again. As I write, I've just booked us all accommodation for our next gig, and I've texted everyone telling them I've found somewhere for us to stay. I'm really looking forward to it. I'm excited – we're going to have a right old laugh, us Fishwives – and I never imagined that would even be possible. But being part of this project, making these friends, pushing through into the unknown – all this has helped put a smile on my face once more. People need a sense of purpose, and this choir has brought us that in abundance.

For this, I thank Colin. I'm indebted to him in so many ways. He gave me a gift when I met him that was beyond marriage and children, the gift that was his love and support and absolute faith in me. Today, in the choir, I feel like he has given me another gift – even in his death.

I'd like to share that gift with you, too, to encourage you to get out there and give singing a go as well. It's so joyous and such a release, and I would love it if my story meant that you tried out your local choir, or even considered setting one up yourself. It's not all about hitting the right notes, as I hope I've shown: it's really about the lovely social interaction.

Remember, music existed long before a music industry. Today, we tend to think that in order to access and enjoy music we have to buy it, consume it – but, as I've learnt, that's just not true. Music is ours already, part of our heritage. Way before record labels existed, ordinary people were using song as a way of sharing stories and binding communities together. I think my story, and that of the Fishwives, demonstrates just how much yearning there is among us to sing together again, heartbeats and breathing in sync, and feel that wonderful sense of togetherness. It's uplifting and healing – and ours to go out and claim as our own.

I do remain changed. And for a time, as you know, my grief transformed me into somebody I didn't want to be, into a version of myself that I didn't like. It took me so long to claw my way back to the person I was. I'm still not quite the same woman I used to be – I never will be – and yet, in some ways I prefer the version of who I am now because I've grown as I could never have imagined I would. I've also learnt to hold things more loosely, to not invest too much emotion or energy in any particular outcome.

Does this mean I no longer hope? No, I am full of plans and dreams. I have just learnt that having something prised from a clenched fist hurts more than allowing it to be taken from an open hand. That's a hard lesson, but one that is worth knowing. I am aware now, also, that pain can leave bitterness in its wake – but it can also increase compassion, empathy and resilience. Every day I hope with all my heart that my beautiful children, who have been robbed of so much, can develop and hold onto these treasures throughout their lives.

There's an easy innocence to life before you experience a trauma – an unconscious feeling of safety and security. It's hard work to rebuild your trust in the world afterwards. So today, I'm far more likely to say, 'Why not us?' than 'Why us?' There's nothing so special about me and my family that we should be singled out for universal protection. But while I don't understand why God allowed what happened to happen, I do trust Him. I think of our lives like the back of a tapestry where we only see the knots, loose threads and castings-off. Maybe only God ever sees the view from the front.

I'll freely admit, I've wanted to be rescued on many an occasion; I've fantasised about someone recognising the hard graft of sole parenting and saying, 'God, you had a tough time. Here's a couple of grand to do the house up,' or, 'Let me take the kids for a weekend so you can have a break.' But I've learnt that, as generous as people can be, ultimately we each have to find a way of rescuing ourselves.

And I know – through experience – that gratitude is a wonderful remedy for self-pity. I always encourage the children and, yes, remind myself to count our blessings, be grateful for small pleasures and be mindful that other people have it far worse. When we cannot change our circumstances, the only power we have is to change our perspective. And if we can imagine it, we can make it real. We can all be free to find out who we have the potential to be, not who we have just had to become. Colin taught me this lesson over and over again.

Despite the pain, the chaos and the loss we've endured, I continue to believe that happiness is a choice – and I choose happiness, for me and for my children.

Of course, there's one last question I should answer. How do I feel about the sea today?

It is what it is: beautiful, powerful, dangerous – and I'll always feel its pull. I think I'll always have to live by the sea, need to feel that crisp breeze, taste the salt in the air, hear the waves break on the shore – and remember Colin, as much a part of this world as the fish in the water or the gulls in the air. Even now I can picture him so clearly, as if it were only yesterday I saw him getting ready for a day's fishing. He puts on his kit, finds some last bit of equipment from his workshop, checks his trailer – gives me a kiss goodbye.

He loved the sea. And if, by some miracle, he could reach me now, from some afterlife, I know that he would still feel the same way.

Acknowledgements

There are several people I would like to publicly acknowledge and recognise here. Writer Emma Rowley for picking up on my blog and my agent Clare Hulton. Without you both, this book would never have happened and your hard work and faith in the story ensured it saw the light of day.

To Amanda Harris at Orion, I am so indebted to you for taking a chance and allowing me the opportunity to share the Fishwives' story. I'm so incredibly grateful to my editor Jillian Young for invaluable guidance and patience with this writing novice whose endless emails must have driven you nuts. Rebecca Gray and Leanne Oliver, thank you both for your encouragement and for so generously sharing your expertise.

Thank you to Tim Jenkins at the Fishermen's Mission and Garry H: you two were with me right from the start of the nightmare and were my rocks in the sea of madness I was almost drowning in at the time. Thank you for helping me manage the horror. To Steve Barber and Sam and Andy Vincett at Southend Vineyard, Steven Hembery, Sylvie Lowe and the members of LRBC and to all in my community, I am forever indebted to you all for showing such compassion and love and seeing us all through the darkest of times. To Julia McM: you helped me more than you could ever know and gave me strategies that pulled me and the kids through the fog, and Rachel Lichenstein for seeing my blog and making me believe I could write.

To my friend Lisa Blatch who introduced me to the work of Southend YMCA and helped give me a reason to get up each day and do something meaningful. For helping through the meltdowns and for all the laughs – my fab SYMCA colleagues especially the wonder woman who is Syrie Cox.

To Mum, Dad, Robin and Siobhan: without family a person is nothing and you and the kids are everything to me. I love you all so very much. To dear Ken: a wise soul and lovely man who I'm privileged to know – I hope this story does justice to the life and memory of your beautiful son. To the Dolby clan: thank you for making me part of the family.

To the MWs: one of you was always at the end of a keyboard, day and night, generously offering comfort, compassion and good solid advice when I was at my loneliest, bereft and most vulnerable.

And lastly but by no means least, for making the music happen: Phil Da Costa, Robin Goodfellow, Jon Cohen, Josh Winiberg, John Puddick, Rob James, John Spurling, Phil Underwood, Russ Strothard, Ian Pearce, Tommy Ludgate and Sarah Grace.

And the wonderful women who make up the Fishwives Choir: Hannah Pascoe, Sue Hendriks, Jenny Ansell, Joy James, Barbara Gallagher, Toni Adams, Didge White, Toni

White, Sharyn Andrews, Mandy Apps, Tracey Edmunds, Jackie Milton, Barbara Bollen, Lee Moulton, Lisa Blatch, Laura Poppy, Lara Hurley, Wendy Roberts, Minghua Zhao, Esther Copote, Holly Lengdon, Michelle Redshaw, Elaine Campbell, Isobel Annett, Debbie Lake, Marlene Hadde, Helen Christie, Yvonne Sheehan, Morna Young, Sarah Richardson, Rachel Thompson and Keri Evans.

To find our more about the work of the Fishermen's Mission please visit:
www.fishermensmission.org.uk

Keep in touch with the Fishwives at:
www.fishwiveschoir.co.uk
www.facebook.com/thefishwiveschoir
Twitter - @fishwiveschoirs

All things are possible in Him.